# STREET ITALIAN 1

## The Best of Italian Slang

# DAVID BURKE

## John Wiley & Sons, Inc.

New York • Chichester • Weinheim • Brisbane • Singapore • Toronto

Design and Production: David Burke
Copy Editor and Translator: Alessio Filippi
Front Cover Illustration: Ty Semaka
Inside Illustrations: Ty Semaka

This book is printed on acid-free paper. ∞

Published by John Wiley & Sons, Inc.
Published simultaneously in Canada

This publication is designed to provide accurate and authoritative
information in regard to the subject matter covered. It is sold with the
understanding that the publisher is not engaged in rendering professional
services. If professional advice or other expert assistance is required, the
services of a competent professional person should be sought.

ISBN 0-471-38438-0

Printed in the United States of America

10 9 8 7 6 5 4 3

This book is dedicated to Noah

# CONTENTS

# ACKNOWLEDGMENTS

I'm forever grateful to Alessio Filippi for his extraordinary contribution to this book. His insight into the spoken Italian language had me constantly amazed. He will always have my deepest appreciation and regard.

To say that Ty Semaka's illustrations are brilliant, hilarious, amazing, and magical would be an understatement. I consider myself so lucky to have found so much talent all wrapped up in one person.

My special thanks and most sincere admiration go to Chris Jackson, my editor at John Wiley & Sons. To date, I don't believe there has been a word or an idiom created that describes someone who is as professional, reassuring, attentive, enthusiastic, motivated, and fun as Chris. He made the entire process truly enjoyable.

I consider myself very fortunate to have been under the wing of so many wonderful people during the creation of this book. A tremendous and warm thanks goes to my pals at John Wiley & Sons: Gerry Helferich, Marcia Samuels, and Sibylle Kazeroid. They are without a doubt the most friendly, supportive, encouraging, and infinitely talented group of people with which I've had the pleasure to work.

# INTRODUCTION

**STREET ITALIAN 1** is the first in a series of entertaining guides that will help you to learn quickly the actual spoken language of Italy that is constantly used in movies, books, and day-to-day business, as well as among family and friends. Now you can finally become an "insider" as you learn the secret world of popular slang that even a ten-year veteran of formalized Italian would not understand!

**STREET ITALIAN 1** is designed to teach the essentials of Italian slang in ten lessons that are divided into five primary parts:

## ■ DIALOGUE

In this section, 20–30 slang words *(shown in boldface)* are presented in an Italian dialogue on the left-hand page. A translation of the dialogue appears on the opposite page. On the following page, you'll find a *literal* translation of the dialogue that often proves to be hilarious!

## ■ VOCABULARY

This section spotlights all of the slang terms that were used in the dialogue and offers:

✔ an example of usage for each entry

✔ an English translation of the example

✔ synonyms, antonyms, variations, or special notes to give you a complete sense of the word or expression.

## ■ PRACTICE THE VOCABULARY

These word games and drills include all of the slang terms and idioms previously learned and will help you test yourself on your comprehension. *(The pages providing the answers to the drills are indicated at the beginning of this section.)*

## ■ DICTATION

This section will allow you to test yourself on your listening comprehension. If you are following along with your cassette, you will hear a series of sentences from the opening dialogue. These sentences will be read by a native speaker at normal conversational speed. When the sentences are read again, there will be a pause after each to give you time to write down what you have heard.

## ■ *REVIEW*

Following each sequence of five chapters is a summary review encompassing all the words and expressions learned up to that point.

The secret to learning **STREET ITALIAN 1** is to follow this simple check-list:

■ Make sure that you have a good grasp on each section before proceeding to the drills. If you've made more than two errors in a particular drill, simply go back and review...then try again! *Remember:* This is a self-paced book, so take your time. You're not fighting the clock!

■ It's very important that you feel comfortable with each chapter before proceeding to the next. Words you've learned along the way may crop up in the following dialogues. So feel comfortable before moving on!

■ Make sure that you read the dialogues and drills aloud. This is an excellent way to become comfortable speaking colloquially and to begin thinking like a native.

**IMPORTANT:**  Slang must always be used with discretion because it is an extremely casual "language" that certainly should not be practiced with formal dignitaries or employers whom you are trying to impress! Most important, since a nonnative speaker of Italian may tend to sound forced or artificial using slang, your first goal should be to *recognize and understand* these types of words. Once you feel that you have a firm grasp on the usage of the slang words and expressions presented in this book, try using some in your conversations for extra color!

Just as a student of formalized English would be rather shocked to run into words like *pooped, zonked,* and *wiped out* and discover that they all go under the heading of "tired," you too will be surprised and amused to encounter a whole new array of terms and phrases usually hidden away in the Italian language and reserved only for the native speaker.

Welcome to the expressive and "colorful" world of slang!

# LEGEND

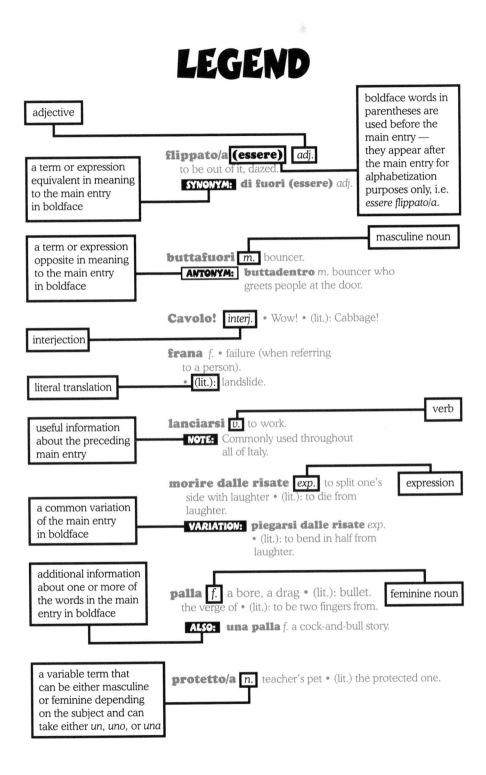

adjective

boldface words in parentheses are used before the main entry — they appear after the main entry for alphabetization purposes only, i.e. *essere flippato/a*.

**flippato/a (essere)** *adj.*
to be out of it, dazed.
**SYNONYM:** **di fuori (essere)** *adj.*

a term or expression equivalent in meaning to the main entry in boldface

masculine noun

a term or expression opposite in meaning to the main entry in boldface

**buttafuori** *m.* bouncer.
**ANTONYM:** **buttadentro** *m.* bouncer who greets people at the door.

**Cavolo!** *interj.* • Wow! • (lit.): Cabbage!

interjection

**frana** *f.* • failure (when referring to a person).
• (lit.): landslide.

literal translation

verb

useful information about the preceding main entry

**lanciarsi** *v.* to work.
**NOTE:** Commonly used throughout all of Italy.

**morire dalle risate** *exp.* to split one's side with laughter • (lit.): to die from laughter.
**VARIATION:** **piegarsi dalle risate** *exp.*
• (lit.): to bend in half from laughter.

expression

a common variation of the main entry in boldface

additional information about one or more of the words in the main entry in boldface

**palla** *f.* a bore, a drag • (lit.): bullet.
the verge of • (lit.): to be two fingers from.
**ALSO:** **una palla** *f.* a cock-and-bull story.

feminine noun

a variable term that can be either masculine or feminine depending on the subject and can take either *un, uno,* or *una*

**protetto/a** *n.* teacher's pet • (lit.) the protected one.

# Per la terza volta questa settimana, Antonio ha *fatto forca* a scuola!

(trans.): For the third time this week, Antonio **cut class**!
(lit.): For the third time this week, Antonio **did the gallows**!

**Antonio:** Tutte le volte che il professore **mi becca** in classe per un'interrogazione, **mi spremo le meningi** per rispondere bene, ma **faccio sempre un buco nell'acqua**.

**Massimo:** Faresti meglio a smettere di **fare forca** a scuola e a cominciare a **sgobbare**, altrimenti mettiti a **fare il ruffiano** con il **prof**. Se **scazzi** il prossimo esame, i tuoi **vecchi** ti **fanno fuori**!

**Antonio:** Lo so. Ma vedi che **casino di roba** ci ha dato da fare durante il fine settimana il nostro prof? Non so come farò a leggere tutte queste **scartoffie** in soli due giorni.

**Massimo:** Eh, lo so. Guarda! Vedi quella gran **bonazza**? Hai sentito l'**ultima** su di lei? Prima era la **protetta** del prof, ma ora non lo è più.

**Antonio:** Perchè? Che è successo?

**Massimo:** Il prof l'ha **presa in castagna** a copiare durante l'esame e ora lui la **sega**.

**Antonio:** **Cavolo**! Sono sbalordito!

# For the third time this week, Antonio *cut class!*

*Antonio:*  Every time the professor **calls on me** in class, I **rack my brain** trying to come up with the right answer, but I always just sit there **stumped**.

*Massimo:*  You'd better stop **cutting class** all the time and start **studying hard** or else **butter up** the **teacher**. If you **blow the next test**, your **parents** are going **to kill** you!

*Antonio:*  I know. Can you believe the **ton of work** the professor gave us to do over the weekend? I don't know how I'm going to read all these darned **books** in just two days.

*Massimo:*  I know what you mean. Look! See that **gorgeous girl**? Did you hear the **news** about her? She used to be the **teacher's pet**, but not anymore.

*Antonio:*  Why? What happened?

*Massimo:*  The professor **caught her in the act** of cheating during the final and he's going to **flunk** her.

*Antonio:*  **Wow**! I'm stunned!

# For the third time this week, Antonio *did the gallows!*

Antonio: Every time the professor **pecks me** in class, I **wring my brain** trying to come up with the right answer, but I always **make a hole in the water**.

Massimo: You'd better stop **doing the gallows** all the time and start **drudging** or else **do the pimp** with the **prof**. If you **"dick" the test**, your **old people** are going **to kill** you!

Antonio: I know. Can you believe the **brothel of stuff** the professor gave us to do over the weekend? I don't know how I'm going to read all these **old papers** in just two days.

Massimo: I know what you mean. Look! See that **really good thing**? Did you hear the **latest** about her? She used to be the **teacher's protected one**, but not anymore.

Antonio: Why? What happened?

Massimo: The professor **took her in the chestnut** for cheating during the final and he's going to **saw her**.

Antonio: **Cabbage**! I'm stunned!

# VOCABULARY

**beccare** *v.* to call on someone in class (said of a teacher) • (lit.): to peck.

> *example:* L'insegnante mi ha **beccato** sei volte oggi e non ho risposto bene nemmeno una volta!
>
> *translation:* The teacher **called on me** six times today and I never got the right answer once!

> **SYNONYM:** **blindare** *v.* • (lit.): to armor (with metal plates).

> **ALSO:** **beccare** *v.* to catch or pick up (an illness, etc.).


**bonazza** *f.* a girl who is extremely pretty to the point of being overdone, "bombshell" (which comes from the adjective *buono/bono [buona/bona]*, meaning "good") • (lit.): a really good thing.

> *example:* L'ex ragazza di Antonio era davvero brutta, ma quella nuova è una gran **bonazza**!
>
> *translation:* Antonio's old girlfriend was really ugly, but his new one is a real **bombshell**!

> **NOTE:** The suffix *-azza* is commonly attached to certain nouns to add a sarcastic connotation.


**casino di roba** *exp.* a lot of stuff • (lit.): a brothel of stuff.

> *example:* Ho portato indietro con me un **casino di roba** dalle vacanze. Sono riuscito a mala pena a fare entrare tutto in valigia!
>
> *translation:* I brought a **ton of stuff** back with me from my vacation. I could hardly fit it all in my suitcase!

> **NOTE:** The noun **roba** can be used in reference to anything unspecific just as "stuff" is used in English.

**Cavolo!** *interj.* Wow! • (lit.): cabbage.

> *example:*   **Cavolo**! Che ragazza stupenda!
>
> *translation:*   **Wow**! What an awesome girl!
>
> **SYNONYM:**   **Capperi!** *interj.* • (lit.): capers.

**fare forca** *exp.* to cut class • (lit.): to do the gallows.

> *example:*   Non ho visto Alberto a scuola oggi. Mi domando se abbia **fatto forca**.
>
> *translation:*   I haven't seen Alberto in school today. I wonder if he **cut class**.
>
> **SYNONYM -1:**   **bigiare** *v.* (Northern Italy)
>
> **SYNONYM -2:**   **bucare** *v.* (Northern & Central Italy) • (lit.): to make a hole (to escape through).
>
> **SYNONYM -3:**   **fare sega** *exp.* (Rome & Central Italy) • (lit.): to do the saw (i.e. to cut out).

**fare fuori** *exp.* to kill, to waste (someone), to take out someone (as in "to kill") • (lit.): to make outside.

> *example:*   Federico ha paura che il ladro lo **faccia fuori**, per il fatto di essere stato testimone oculare del furto.
>
> *translation:*   Federico is scared that the thief is going **to kill him** for witnessing the crime.
>
> **SYNONYM -1:**   **far la festa a qualcuno** *exp.* • (lit.): to give someone a (good-bye) party.
>
> **SYNONYM -2:**   **fare secco qualcuno** *exp.* • (lit.): to make someone dry.
>
> **SYNONYM -3:**   **fare una frittata** *exp.* • (lit.): to make an omelette out of someone.
>
> **SYNONYM -4:**   **stendere qualcuno** *exp.* • (lit.): to lay someone down.

**fare il ruffiano/la ruffiana** *exp.* to butter someone up • (lit.): to do like a pimp/madame.

> *example:*   Marco **fa il ruffiano** con il capo perchè ha intenzione di chiedergli un aumento.
>
> *translation:*   Marco is **buttering up** the boss because he's going to ask him for a raise.

**fare un buco nell'acqua** *exp.* to be totally unsuccessful, to botch up something • (lit.): to make a hole in the water.

> *example:* Ogni volta che provo ad aggiustare la mia macchina, **faccio un buco nell'acqua**. La prossima volta vado da un meccanico!
>
> *translation:* Every time I try to fix my car, **I botch it up**. Next time, I'm going to a mechanic!
>
> **ALSO:** **tappare un buco** *exp.* to pay a debt • (lit.): to fill a hole.

**prendere in castagna** *exp.* to catch someone in the act • (lit.): to take in the chestnut.

> *example:* Ho **preso** Luigi **in castagna**, mentre cercava di rubare la mia bici.
>
> *translation:* I **caught Luigi in the act** of trying to steal my bicycle!
>
> **SYNONYM -1:** **esser colto/a in flagrante** *exp.* • (lit.): to be caught in the flagrant [action].
>
> **SYNONYM -2:** **esser colto/a sul fatto** *exp.* • (lit.): to be caught in the fact.

**prof** *m. & f.* professor, teacher • (lit.): prof.

> *example:* Hai visto la nostra nuova **prof**? È bellissima!
>
> *translation:* Did you see our new **prof**? She's absolutely beautiful!
>
> **NOTE:** Although the academic term for professor is either **professore** *m.* or **professoressa** *f.* depending on the sex, the abbreviated form **prof** is both masculine and feminine.

**protetto/a** *n.* teacher's pet • (lit.): protected one (from the verb *proteggere*, meaning "to protect").

> *example:* L'unico motivo per cui Francesca prende dei buoni voti è perchè lei è la **protetta** dell'insegnante.
>
> *translation:* The only reason Francesca gets good grades is because she's the **teacher's pet**.

**scartoffie** *f.pl.* a contemptuous term for schoolbooks, "darned books" • (lit.): old papers.

> *example:* Devo cancellare la mia vacanza perchè devo leggere tutte queste **scartoffie** entro venerdì prossimo!
>
> *translation:* I have to cancel my vacation because I need to read all these **darned books** by next Friday!

**scazzare** *v.* to blow it • (lit.): to "dick" something up.

> *example:* Ho davvero **scazzato** l'esame! So che non passerò!
>
> *translation:* I totally **messed up on** the test! I know I'm not going to pass!
>
> **NOTE:** This comes from the masculine noun *cazzo*, meaning "penis" or, more closely, "dick." It is included here because of its extreme popularity.
>
> **SYNONYM:** **fare una cappella** *exp.* • (lit.): to do a mushroom cap.

**segare** *v.* to fail someone • (lit.): to cut with a saw.

> *example:* Il professore mi ha detto che mi **sega** alla fine dell'anno, se non passo il prossimo esame!
>
> *translation:* The professor said he would **fail me** at the end of the school year if I didn't pass the next test!
>
> **SYNONYM -1:** **bocciare** *v.* • (lit.): to knock away the opponent's wood in the game of bocce.
>
> **SYNONYM -2:** **fregare** *v.* *(Northern & Central Italy)* • (lit.): to rub.
>
> **SYNONYM -3:** **gambizzare** *v.* (from the feminine noun *gamba*, meaning "leg" – therefore the literal translation could be "to cut someone's legs off so that he/she can no longer continue.")

**sgobbare** *v.* to work hard (from *gobba*, meaning "hump," representing a heavy load being carried on one's shoulders or back).

> *example:* Mi piacerebbe andare al cinema con te, ma devo **sgobbare** tutta la notte. Devo presentare una grossa relazione domani mattina.
>
> *translation:* I'd like to go with you to the movies, but I have **to work hard** all night. I'm giving a big presentation tomorrow morning.
>
> **NOTE:** sgobbo *m.* work • *andare allo sgobbo;* to go to work.

**spremersi le meningi** *exp.* to rack one's brain • (lit.): to wring one's brain (from the Greek word *meninx*, meaning "brain").

> *example:* Come si chiama tua sorella? Ho **spremuto invano le mie meningi** per cercare di ricordarlo!

> *translation:* What is your sister's name? I've been **racking my brain** trying to remember it!

> **SYNONYM:** **rompersi la testa** *exp.* • (lit.): to break one's head.

**ultima** *f.* news • (lit.): last (or the "latest").

> *example:* Hai sentito l'**ultima**? Massimo si sposa la prossima settimana!

> *translation:* Did you hear the **news**? Massimo is getting married next week!

**vecchi** *m.pl.* parents, "folks" • (lit.): old people.

> *example:* Vado a Firenze per passare le vacanze con i miei **vecchi**.

> *translation:* I'm going to Florence to spend the holiday with my **folks**.

> **NOTE:** **vecchio** *m.* father • (lit.): old man / **vecchia** *f.* mother • (lit.): old lady.

# PRACTICE THE VOCABULARY

*(Answers to Lesson One, p. 175)*

## A. Underline the word that best completes the phrase.

1. Ho portato indietro con me un (**casino**, **carino**, **casinò**) di roba dalle vacanze. Sono riuscito a mala pena a fare entrare tutto in valigia!

2. L'insegnante mi ha (**steccato**, **abbinato**, **beccato**) sei volte oggi e non ho risposto bene nemmeno una volta!

3. Come si chiama tua sorella? Ho spremuto invano le mie (**meningi**, **meringhe**, **sfingi**) per cercare di ricordare il suo nome!

4. Devo cancellare la mia vacanza perchè devo leggere tutte queste (**scartoffie**, **scatole**, **buffe**) entro venerdì prossimo!

5. Non ho visto Alberto a scuola oggi. Mi domando se abbia fatto (**barca**, **porta**, **forca**).

6. Hai sentito (**la prima**, **l'ultima**, **la penultima**)? Massimo si sposa la prossima settimana!

7. Vado a Firenze per passare le vacanze con i miei (**vecchi**, **secchi**, **venti**).

8. Il professore mi ha detto che mi (**sera**, **sega**, **saga**) alla fine dell'anno, se non passo il prossimo esame!

9. L'unico motivo per cui Francesca prende dei buoni voti è perchè lei è la (**protetta**, **barchetta**, **promessa**) dell'insegnante!

10. Marco fa il (**ruspante**, **anziano**, **ruffiano**) con il capo, perchè ha intenzione di chiedergli un aumento.

# B. Complete the phrases below by choosing the appropriate words from the list.

**BECCA**  
**SEGA**  
**BONAZZA**  
**BUCO**  
**CASTAGNA**

**CAVOLO**  
**FUORI**  
**RUFFIANA**  
**SCAZZATO**  
**SGOBBARE**

1. L'ex ragazza di Antonio era davvero brutta, ma quella nuova è una gran _____!

2. _____! Che ragazza stupenda!

3. Federico ha paura che il ladro lo faccia _____, per il fatto di essere stato testimone oculare del furto.

4. Mi piacerebbe andare al cinema con te, ma devo _____ tutta la notte. Devo presentare una grossa relazione domani mattina.

5. Il professore mi ha detto che mi _____ alla fine dell'anno, se non passo il prossimo esame!

6. Ho davvero _____ l'esame! So che non passerò!

7. Ho preso Luigi in _____, mentre cercava di rubare la mia bici.

8. Ogni volta che provo ad aggiustare la mia macchina, faccio un _____ nell'acqua. La prossima volta vado da un meccanico!

9. Tutte le volte che il prof _____ Francesca, lei ha sempre la risposta giusta.

10. È ovvio che Simona fa la _____ con il professore perchè vuole prendere un bel voto.

## C. Match the English phrase in the left column with the Italian translation from the right. Write the appropriate letter in the box.

☐ 1. If I come home late, my mother is going **to kill** me!

☐ 2. The police officer **caught him in the act of stealing**.

☐ 3. **Wow**! I can't believe it!

☐ 4. What's that girl's name? I've been **racking my brain** trying to remember.

☐ 5. I tried to fix my television but I **really blew it**.

☐ 6. I wish I could go with you tonight, but I have **a ton** of work I need to finish.

☐ 7. Antonella brings the teacher a gift every day! That's why she's the **teacher's pet**.

☐ 8. The teacher **flunked** Matteo? He must have really done badly on the test!

☐ 9. I don't understand it. Roberto never **studies hard**, but he always gets a perfect score on the tests.

☐ 10. I'll never be able to read all these **darned books** in just two days!

A. **Cavolo**! Non posso crederci!

B. L'insegnante ha **segato** Matteo? Deve aver fatto veramente male l'esame.

C. Non capisco. Roberto non **sgobba** mai, ma prende sempre il massimo dei voti negli esami.

D. Ho cercato di aggiustare il mio televisore, ma ho **fatto un buco nell'acqua**.

E. Se torno a casa tardi, mia madre mi **fa fuori**!

F. Vorrei uscire con te stasera, ma ho **un casino** di lavoro che devo finire.

G. L'agente di polizia lo ha **preso in castagna**.

H. Antonella porta un regalo all'insegnante tutti i giorni. Ecco perchè è la **protetta del prof**.

I. Non riuscirò mai a finire di leggere queste **scartoffie** in due giorni!

J. Come si chiama quella ragazza? Mi sono **spremuto le meningi**, cercando di ricordare.

## D. CROSSWORD
### Fill in the crossword puzzle on page 21 by choosing from the words in the list below.

| | |
|---|---|
| **ACQUA** | **PROF** |
| **BECCARE** | **PROTETTO** |
| **BONAZZA** | **RUFFIANO** |
| **CASINO** | **SCARTOFFIE** |
| **CASTAGNA** | **SCAZZARE** |
| **CAVOLO** | **SEGARE** |
| **FORCA** | **SGOBBARE** |
| **FUORI** | **ULTIMA** |
| **MENINGI** | **VECCHI** |

## ACROSS

16. _____! *interj.* Wow! • (lit.): cabbage.

17. **fare un buco nell'**_____ *exp.* to be totally unsuccessful, to botch up something • (lit.): to make a hole in the water.

22. _____ *v.* to blow it • (lit.): to "dick" something up.

43. _____ *f.pl.* contemptuous name given to schoolbooks, "darned books" • (lit.): old papers.

48. **spremersi le** _____ *exp.* to rack one's brain • (lit.): to wring one's brain (from the Greek word *meninx*, meaning "brain").

53. _____ *v.* to fail someone • (lit.): to cut with a saw.

## DOWN

1. _____ *m.pl.* parents, "folks" • (lit.): old people.

7. _____ *v.* to call on someone in class (said of a teacher) • (lit.): to catch.

11. _____ *v.* to work hard.

14. _____ *f.* a girl who is extremely pretty to the point of being overdone, "bombshell" (from the adjective *bono/a*, meaning "good") • (lit.): a really good thing.

15. **fare** _____ *exp.* to kill, to waste (someone), to take out someone (as in "to kill") • (lit.): to make outside.

23. **fare il** _____ *exp.* to butter someone up • (lit.): to do like a pimp.

32. **prendere in** _____ *exp.* to catch someone in the act • (lit.): to take in the chestnut.

35. _____ *n.* teacher's pet • (lit.): protected one (from the verb *proteggere*, meaning "to protect").

38. _____ *m. & f.* professor, teacher • (lit.): prof.

39. _____ *f.* news • (lit.): last (or the "latest").

40. _____ **di roba** *exp.* a lot of stuff • (lit.): a brothel of stuff.

44. **fare** _____ *exp.* to cut class • (lit.): to do the gallows.

# CROSSWORD PUZZLE

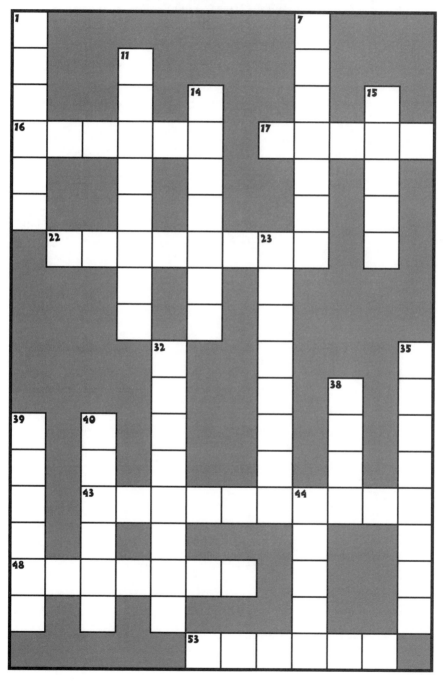

# E. DICTATION
## Test Your Listening Comprehension

*(This dictation can be found in the Appendix on page 193.)*

If you are following along with your cassette, you will now hear a series of sentences from the opening dialogue. These sentences will be read by a native speaker at normal conversational speed (which may seem fast to you at first). In addition, the words will be pronounced as you would actually hear them in a conversation, often including some common reductions.

The first time the sentences are presented, simply listen in order to get accustomed to the speed and heavy use of reductions. The sentences will then be read again with a pause after each to give you time to write down what you heard. The third time the sentences are read, follow along with what you have written.

# Francesca *ha una cotta* per Giovanni!

*(trans.): Francesca **has a crush** on Giovanni!*
*(lit.): Francesca **has a baking** for Giovanni!*

**Simona:** Dove vai, così tutta **tirata**? Che fai? Esci con un **tipo** nuovo?

**Francesca:** Lui non è certamente il mio ragazzo! Vado a cena fuori con Giovanni Papini.

**Simona:** Vuoi dire con quel **lungagnone** che si mette sempre quei **cenci** larghi addosso? È un **secchionaccio della madonna**! Ieri in classe ha fatto questa noiosissima presentazione, e per tutto il tempo **aveva la bottega aperta**. Sono **morta dalle risate**! Non mi dire che **hai una bella cotta per quello**!

**Francesca:** Eh, sì, **buona notte**! Tutte le volte che lo vedo avvicinarsi a me, cerco di **seminarlo**, ma lui mi blocca sempre. Mi ha **scocciato** per un mese chiedendomi di uscire, così alla fine gli ho detto di sì. Stasera sarà una **palla** indescrivibile.

**Simona:** Di solito lui è così teso. Mi sorprende che questa volta abbia avuto il coraggio di **lanciarsi**. Forse questa volta riuscirà a convincerti!

**Francesca:** Ma tu sei **di fuori**!

**Simona:** Forse, ma se ti vedo tornare con un **succhiotto** al collo, vuol dire che la vostra serata è stata una **bomba**!

**Francesca:** Ha, ha, molto spiritosa! Che fortuna se mi **tirasse un bidone**!

# Francesca *has* a crush on Giovanni!

*Simona:* Where are you going all **dressed up**? What's up? Are you going out with a new **boyfriend**?

*Francesca:* He's definitely not my boyfriend! I'm going to dinner with Giovanni Papini.

*Simona:* You mean the **tall and lanky person** who always wears **gross-looking clothes** that are too big for him?! He's **a really nerdy bookworm type**. Yesterday in class, he gave this long, boring speech and the entire time **his fly was open**. I **died laughing**! Don't tell me you're **head over heels** for him!

*Francesca:* **No way**! Every time I see him walking towards me, I try **to ditch him** but he always corners me. He's been **bugging** me for a date for a month, so I finally said okay. This evening is going to be such a **drag**.

*Simona:* He's usually so uptight. I'm surprised he actually got the courage **to make the move**. Maybe he'll eventually win you over.

*Francesca:* Are you **out of your mind**?

*Simona:* Well, if you come back with a **hickey**, I'll know you had a **blast**!

*Francesca:* Ha, ha. Very funny. Maybe I'll be lucky and he'll **stand me up**!

# Francesca *has* a baking for Giovanni!

*Simona:* Where are you going all **pulled**? What are you doing? Are you going out with a new **guy**?

*Francesca:* He's definitely not my boyfriend! I'm going to dinner with Giovanni Papini.

*Simona:* You mean the **beanpole** who always wears pieces of **cloth** that are too big for him?! He's **a nerdy bookworm of the Madonna**. Yesterday in class, he gave this long, boring speech and the entire time **his shop was open**. I **died of laughter**! Don't tell me you have **a baking** for him!

*Francesca:* Oh, yes, **good night**! Every time I see him walking toward me, I try **to seed him** but he always corners me. He's been **breaking my eggshell** for a date for a month, so I finally said okay. This evening is going to be such a **ball**.

*Simona:* He's usually so uptight. I'm surprised he actually got the courage to ask you out. Maybe he'll eventually win you over.

*Francesca:* Are you **out**?

*Simona:* Well, if you come back with a **sucked thing**, I'll know you had a **bomb**!

*Francesca:* Ha, ha. Very funny. Maybe I'll be lucky and he'll **throw me a trash can**!

# VOCABULARY

**bomba** f. a blast (of fun) • (lit.): a bomb.

>   *example:*   Mi sont divertito moltissimo al Luna Park. Che **bomba**!
>   *translation:*   I had a great time at the amusement park. What a **blast**!

>   **SYNONYM:**   **cannonata** f. • (lit.): cannon shot.
>   **ALSO:**   **una bomba** f. a tall tale or lie.
>   **NOTE:**   **tirare una bomba** exp. to tell a lie • (lit.): to pull a bomb.

**bottega aperta (avere la)** exp. to have one's zipper open unintentionally • (lit.): to have one's shop open.

>   *example:*   L'insegnante **ha la bottega aperta**! Mi domando se qualcuno in classe avrà il coraggio di dirglielo!
>   *translation:*   The teacher's **fly is open**! I wonder if anyone in the class will have the nerve to tell him!

**Buona notte!** interj. No way! You've got to be kidding! Oh, brother! • (lit.): Good night!

>   *example:*   Simona esce con Marco? **Buona notte**! Lui ha il doppio degli anni di lei!
>   *translation:*   Simona is dating Marco? **Oh, brother**! He's twice as old as she is!

>   **SYNONYM:**   **Non esiste!** interj. • (lit.): It doesn't exist!

**cenci** m.pl. ugly clothing • (lit.): piece of cloth (from the masculine noun cencio, meaning "cloth").

>   *example:*   Hai visto i **cenci** che Carolina aveva addosso alla festa? Era ridicola!
>   *translation:*   Did you see the **ugly clothes** Carolina was wearing to the party? She looked ridiculous!

>   **SYNONYM:**   **non essere nei propri cenci** exp. to feel out of it, out of sorts • (lit.): not to be in one's clothes.

**cotta per qualcuno (avere una)** *exp.* to have a crush on someone • (lit.): to have a baking for someone (from the feminine noun *cottura*,
meaning "cooking" or "baking").

> *example:*    Credo che Giovanni **abbia una cotta per me**, per-
> chè mi segue ovunque!
>
> *translation:*  I think Giovanni **has a crush on me**, because he
> follows me everywhere!

> **VARIATION:**  **prendere una cotta per qualcuno** *exp.* • (lit.): to
> take a baking for someone.

> **NOTE:**  **Sono cotto per lei** ("I am baked for her") [or] **Ho
> una cotta per lei** ("I have a baking for her") – Note
> that cotta is an adjective in the first example (which is
> why it changed to *cotto*) and is a noun in the second
> example (which is why it remains *cotta* even if said by a
> man).

> **SYNONYM -1:**  **avere una fissa per qualcuno** *exp.* • (lit.): to have
> an obsession for someone.

> > **NOTE:**  The feminine adjective *fissa* is an abbreviation
> > of *fissazione*, meaning "obsession."

> **SYNONYM -2:**  **prendere una scuffia per qualcuno** *exp.* • (lit.):
> to take a capsizing for someone.

**della madonna** *exp.* big-time, in a major way • (lit.): of the Madonna.

> *example:*    Francesca mi ha detto di avere sangue blu. Lei è una
> bugiarda **della madonna**.
>
> *translation:*  Francesca told me that she comes from royalty. She's
> **such a big-time** liar.

> **NOTE:**  In the example above, *sangue blu* (literally translated as
> "blue blood") was used to mean "royalty" just as it is in
> English.

> **SYNONYM -1:**  **alla grande** *exp.* • (lit.): to the big.

> **SYNONYM -2:**  **il massimo / la massima** *exp.* • (lit.): the maximum
> • *Questa pizza è il massimo!;* This pizza is the best!

**di fuori (essere)** *exp.* to be crazy • (lit.): to be out (of one's mind).

> *example:*    Hai guidato senza occhiali? Sei **fuori di testa**?
> Avresti potuto fare un incidente!
>
> *translation:*  You drove me without your glasses? Are you **out of
> your mind**? You could have gotten into an accident!

**SYNONYM -1:** **flippato/a** *adj.* • (lit.): flipped.

**SYNONYM -2:** **girare** *v.* (Central Italy) • (lit.): to turn • *Ma ti gira il cervello?*; Are you nuts? (lit.): Is your brain turning?

**lanciarsi** *v.* to get the courage to do something, to get up one's nerve
• (lit.): to hurl oneself.

> *example:* Quella ragazza mi piace molto. Devo **lanciarmi** per-
> chè voglio invitarla ad uscire con me.
>
> *translation:* I really like that girl. I need to **get up my nerve**
> because I want to invite her to go out with me.
>
> **ALSO:** **lanciare un'idea** *exp.* to make a suggestion • (lit.): to
> throw an idea.

**lungagnone** *m.* a tall and lanky person (from the adjective *lungo,* meaning "long," "tall," etc.), "beanpole."

> *example:* Davide, da bambino era basso e grassottello. Ora
> invece è un **lungagnone**!
>
> *translation:* When David was a little boy, he was short and over-
> weight. Now he's a **beanpole**!

**SYNONYM -1:** **pertica** *f.* • (lit.): pole.

**SYNONYM -2:** **perticone** *m.* from *pertica,* meaning "long pole."

**SYNONYM -3:** **stanga** *f.* • (lit.): bar.

**morire dalle risate** *exp.* to split one's sides with laughter • (lit.): to die
from laughter.

> *example:* That movie was hilarious! I thought I was going **to die
> laughing**!
>
> *translation:* Quel film era buffissimo! Pensavo di **morire dalle
> risate**!

**VARIATION -1:** **piegarsi dalle risate** *exp.* • (lit.): to bend in half
from laughter.

**VARIATION -2:** **sganasciarsi dal ridere** *exp.* • (lit.): to dislocate
one's jaw from laughing.

**VARIATION -3:** **sganasciarsi dalle risate** *exp.* • (lit.): to dislocate
one's jaw from laughter.

**VARIATION -4:** **sganasciarsi per le risate** *exp.* • (lit.): to dislocate
one's jaw for laughing.

**palla** *f.* a bore, a drag • (lit.): bullet, ball.

> *example:* Ho passato tutta la vacanza al chiuso, perchè non ha fatto altro che piovere. Che **palla**!

> *translation:* I spent my entire vacation inside because it never stopped raining. My vacation was a **bore**!

> **NOTE:** The literal meaning of **palla** is "ball" which should not be mistaken for the slang meaning of "ball" (meaning "a lot of fun" or "a blast"). In fact, its meaning is exactly the opposite! For example: *Che palla!* = What a bore! (Not "What a blast!").

> **SYNONYM -1:** **depressione** *f.* said of anything boring and dull • (lit.): depression.

> **SYNONYM -2:** **piaga** *f.* (Northern & Central Italy) • (lit.): plague.

> **SYNONYM -3:** **pizza** *f.*

> **ALSO:** **una palla** / **una balla** *f.* a cock-and-bull story.

**scocciare qualcuno** *v.* to bug someone • (lit.): to break (an eggshell).

> *example:* Smettila di farmi tutte queste domande! Mi stai **scocciando**!

> *translation:* Stop asking me so many questions! You're **bugging** me!

> **SYNONYM -1:** **bombardare qualcuno** *v.* • (lit.): to bombard or shell someone.

> **SYNONYM -2:** **tafanare** *v.* from *tafano,* meaning "horsefly."

> **SYNONYM -3:** **stare sui calli a qualcuno** *exp.* • (lit.): to be on someone's corns.

**secchionaccio** *m.* nerdy bookworm.

> *example:* Fernando non studia mai, mentre suo fratello è un **secchionaccio**.

> *translation:* Fernando never studies but his brother is a **nerdy bookworm**.

> **NOTE:** The masculine noun **secchionaccio** is a stronger form of **secchione/sechia**, meaning "nerdy, bookworm type."

**seminare qualcuno** v. to ditch someone • (lit.): to sow or seed someone.

>*example:* Il mio fratellino ci veniva dietro da tutte le parti, ma alla fine lo abbiamo **seminato** quando siamo entrati al cinema.
>
>*translation:* My little brother was following us around everywhere, so we finally **ditched** him when we went to the movies.

>**SYNONYM:** **tagliare** v. • (lit.): to cut.
>
>>**NOTE:** *"Taglia!"* is also used to mean "Wrap it up!" as in "Wrap up the conversation!"

**succhiotto** m. hickey • (lit.): (from the verb *succhiare,* meaning "to suck") a "sucked thing."

>*example:* Simona ieri sera è tornata a casa con un **succhiotto** sul collo! Immagino che si sia divertita con Roberto!
>
>*translation:* Simona came home last night with a **hickey** on her neck! I guess she had a good time with Roberto!

**tipo** m. guy, "dude" • (lit.): type, species.

>*example:* Conosci quel **tipo**? Io non l'ho mai visto prima.
>
>*translation:* Do you know that **guy**? I've never seen him before.

>**NOTE:** **tipa** f. girl, "chick" • (lit.): type, species.

**tirare un bidone** exp. to stand someone up on a date • (lit.): to throw a trash can.

>*example:* Ho aspettato Alessio per un'ora! Credo che mi abbia **tirato un bidone**!
>
>*translation:* I've been waiting an hour for Alessio to arrive! I think he **stood me up**!

>**VARIATION:** **fare un bidone** exp. • (lit.): to do/to make a trash can.

>**SYNONYM:** **dare buca** exp. • (lit.): to give hole.

**tirato/a** adj. dressed up • (lit.): pulled (together).

>*example:* Stai benissimo! Non ti avevo mai visto così **tirato**!
>
>*translation:* You look great! I've never seen you so **dressed up** before!

# PRACTICE THE VOCABULARY

*(Answers to Lesson Two, p. 177)*

## A. Match the English phrase in the left column with the Italian translation from the right. Write the appropriate letter in the box.

☐ 1. Did you see the ugly clothes Manuela was wearing today? They were so ugly!

☐ 2. Luigi dyed his hair orange? Oh, brother!

☐ 3. Gianni sits around and watches television all day. He's big-time lazy!

☐ 4. Ilaria has a crush on Massimo!

☐ 5. You can't drive in your condition! Are you out of your mind?

☐ 6. Giacomo and Mariella are an interesting couple. He's a beanpole and she's extremely fat!

☐ 7. Your father told me the funniest joke. I thought I was going to die laughing.

☐ 8. Stop asking me so many questions. You're really bugging me!

A. Luigi si è tinto i capelli d'arancione? **Buona notte**!

B. Ilaria **ha una cotta per** Massimo!

C. Hai visto che **cenci** aveva addosso Manuela, oggi? Erano orribili!

D. Tuo padre mi ha raccontato una barzelletta buffissima. Pensavo di **morire dalle risate**.

E. Non puoi quidare nelle tue condizioni! Sei **fuori di testa**?

F. Smettila di farmi tante domande. Mi **stai** davvero **scocciando**!

G. Giacomo e Mariella sono una coppia interessante. Lui è un **lungagnone**, mentre lei è grassissima!

H. Gianni sta seduto a guardare la televisione tutto il giorno. È un pigro **della madonna**!

## B. Complete the following phrases by choosing the appropriate word(s) from the list below. Make all necessary changes.

**BOMBA**        **PALLA**
**BOTTEGA**      **SEMINATO**
**COTTA**        **SUCCHIOTTO**
**LANCIARMI**    **TIPO**
**NOTTE**        **TIRATO**

1. Mi diverto moltissimo al Luna Park. Che _____!

2. Simona esce con Marco? Buona _____! Lui ha il doppio degli anni di lei!

3. Simona ieri sera è tornata a casa con un _____ sul collo! Immagino che si sia divertita con Roberto!

4. L'insegnante ha la _____ aperta! Mi domando se qualcuno in classe avrà il coraggio di dirglielo!

5. Conosci quel _____? Io non l'ho mai visto prima.

6. Stai benissimo! Non ti avevo mai visto così _____!

7. Ho passato tutta la vacanza al chiuso, perchè non ha fatto altro che piovere. Che _____!

8. Il mio fratellino ci veniva dietro da tutte le parti, ma alla fine lo abbiamo _____ quando siamo entrati al cinema.

9. Quella ragazza mi piace molto! Devo _____ perchè voglio invitarla ad uscire con me!

10. Credo che Giovanni abbia una _____ per me, perchè mi segue ovunque!

# C. Underline the correct definition.

1. **seminare qualcuno:**
   a. to ditch someone
   b. to bump into someone

2. **tipo:**
   a. difficult job
   b. guy

3. **bomba:**
   a. bad movie or play
   b. blast (of fun)

4. **bottega aperta (avere la):**
   a. to keep late hours, to work overtime
   b. to have one's zipper open

5. **cenci:**
   a. ugly clothing
   b. old car, jalopy

6. **Buona notte!**
   a. Good grief!
   b. Leave me alone!

7. **succhiotto:**
   a. hickey
   b. sucker

8. **tirare un bidone**
   a. to stand someone up on a date
   b. to get extremely angry

9. **cotta per qualcuno (avere una)**
   a. to have a crush on someone
   b. to overcook something

10. **della madonna:**
    a. unique
    b. big-time

11. **tirato/a:**
    a. dressed up
    b. stressed out

12. **di fuori (essere)**
    a. to be stood up on a date
    b. to be crazy

13. **morire dalle risate:**
    a. to die of laughter
    b. to die of hunger

14. **lanciarsi:**
    a. to get up one's nerve
    b. to give up

15. **lungagnone:**
    a. a tall, thin person, a "beanpole"
    b. a genius

16. **palla:**
    a. a bore
    b. said of something exciting

17. **scocciare qualcuno:**
    a. to excite someone
    b. to bug someone

18. **secchionaccio:**
    a. bad food
    b. a nerdy bookworm

## D. Complete the dialogue using the list below.

| | |
|---|---|
| **BIDONE** | **NOTTE** |
| **BOMBA** | **PALLA** |
| **BOTTEGA** | **RISATE** |
| **CENCI** | **SCOCCIATO** |
| **COTTA** | **SECCHIONACCIO** |
| **FUORI** | **SEMINARLO** |
| **LANCIARSI** | **SUCCHIOTTO** |
| **LUNGAGNONE** | **TIPO** |
| **MADONNA** | **TIRATA** |

*Simona:*      Dove vai, così tutta _____? Che fa? Esci con un

            _____ nuovo?

*Francesca:*    Lui non è certamente il mio ragazzo! Vado a cena fuori con

            Giovanni Papini.

*Simona:*      Vuoi dire con quel _____ che si mette sempre

            quei _____ larghi addosso? È un _____

            della _____! Ieri in classe ha fatto questa

            noiosissima presentazione, e per tutto il tempo aveva la

            _____ aperta. Mi sono talmente sganasciata dalle

            _____ che pensavo di morire. Non mi dire che hai

            una bella _____ per quello!

*Francesca:*    Eh, sì, buona _____! Tutte le volte che lo vedo

            avvicinarsi a me, cerco di _____, ma lui mi blocca

sempre. Mi ha _____ per un mese,

chiedendomi di uscire, così alla fine gli ho detto di sì. Stasera

sarà una _____ indescrivibile!

Simona:        Di solito lui è così teso. Mi sorprende che questa volta abbia

avuto il coraggio di _____. Forse questa volta

riuscirà a convincerti!

Francesca:     Ma tu sei di _____!

Simona:        Forse, ma se ti vedo tornare con un _____al

collo, vuol dire che la vostra serata è stata una _____!

Francesca:     Ha, ha, molto spiritosa! Che fortuna se mi tirasse un

_____!

# E. DICTATION
## Test Your Listening Comprehension

*(This dictation can be found in the Appendix on page 193.)*

If you are following along with your cassette, you will now hear a series of sentences from the opening dialogue. These sentences will be read by a native speaker at normal conversational speed (which may seem fast to you at first). In addition, the words will be pronounced as you would actually hear them in a conversation, often including some common reductions.

The first time the sentences are presented, simply listen in order to get accustomed to the speed and heavy use of reductions. The sentences will then be read again with a pause after each to give you time to write down what you heard. The third time the sentences are read, follow along with what you have written.

WILL WORK FOR SCRATCH

# Pasquale si è *spennato* a forza di fare sempre benzina!

(trans.): Pasquale went **broke** buying gas all the time!
(lit.): Pasquale got **plucked** buying gas all the time!

*Salvatore:* **Ammazza**! Che è, la tua macchina nuova? È davvero **spaziale**! Che è successo alla tua vecchia **carcassa**?

*Pasquale:* Una vecchia **babbiona** tirava dritto giù per strada e mi ha **bocciato** con la sua macchina. Ho **avuto un bel culo** che non mi ha **spappolato**! In ogni caso, la mia vecchia macchina è **kaput** ormai da una settimana e così ho comprato questa incredibile **bomba** che **va come le sassate**. Fortunatamente questa non **succhia** come quella vecchia. Pensavo che mi sarei **spennato** a forza di fare sempre benzina. Salta su, che ti do uno **strappo**. Non hai idea di quanto **scheggi** questa macchina e delle **sgommate** che ci faccio.

*Salvatore:* **Occhio** però, a non farti **stoppare** dalla **pula** e a non finire **al fresco** per eccesso di velocità!

# Pasquale went broke buying gas all the time!

*Salvatore:* **Wow**! Is that your new car? It's **awesome**! What happened to your **old wreck**?

*Pasquale:* Some **old geezer** was driving down the street and **bashed into** me with her car. I was **really lucky** that she didn't **kill me**! Anyway, my poor car's been **broken down** for a week, so I bought this new **incredible car** that **flies**. Fortunately it doesn't **guzzle up gas** like my old one. I thought I was going to go **broke** buying gas all the time. Jump in and I'll give you a **lift**. You won't believe how this car can **rev up** and **burn rubber**.

*Salvatore:* **Watch out** that you don't get **stopped** by a **cop** and end up **in the cooler** for speeding!

# Pasquale got *plucked* buying gas all the time!

*Salvatore:* **Killer**! Is that your new car? It's **spacial**! What happened to your old **carcass**?

*Pasquale:* Some **old woman** was driving down the street and **knocked into** me with her car. I had **a handsome ass** that she didn't **crush me**! Anyway, my poor car's been **kaput** for a week, so I bought this new **bomb** that **goes like thrown rocks**. Fortunately it doesn't **suck [gas]** like my old one. I thought I was going to be **plucked** doing gas all the time. Jump in and I'll give you a **tear**! You won't believe how this baby can **splinter** and **make tire tracks**.

*Salvatore:* **Eye** that you don't get **stopped** by the **husk** and end up **in the cool place** for speeding!

# VOCABULARY

**al fresco** *adv.* in jail, in the "cooler" • (lit.): in the cool [place].

    *example:* Il rapinatore passerà cinque anni **al fresco**.

    *translation:* The robber is going to spend five years in the **cooler**.

**Ammazza!** *interj.* Wow! • (lit.): from the verb *ammazzare*, meaning "to kill" – therefore the closest literal translation could be "Killer!"

    *example:* **Ammazza**! Hai visto quella stella cadente? Era così luminosa!

    *translation:* **Wow**! Did you see that shooting star? It was so bright!

    **SYNONYM -1:** **Ammappa!** *interj.*

    **SYNONYM -2:** **Capperi** *interj.* • (lit.): capers.

    **SYNONYM -3:** **Uah!** *interj.* a variation of the English "Wow!"

    **SYNONYM -4:** **Wow!** *interj.* (from English)

**andare come le sassate** *exp.* to be extremely fast, to go as fast as a rocket • (lit.): to go like thrown stones or projectiles.

    *example:* Non riesco a credere come la gente guidi in questa città. **Vanno tutti come le sassate**!

    *translation:* I can't believe the way people drive in this city. **They all drive like bats out of hell**!

    **NOTE:** The masculine noun *sasso* means "stone." However, when the same stone is thrown, it is called *una sassata*, meaning "a thrown stone."

**babbiona** *f.* crotchety old woman, old geezer.

    *example:* La mia prima maestra di pianoforte era una [vecchia] **babbiona** che mi faceva suonare musica che odiavo. Ora ho una maestra giovane che mi fa suonare quello che voglio!

    *translation:* The first piano teacher I ever had was this [old] **geezer** who made me play music I hated. Now I have a young teacher who lets me play whatever I want!

**NOTE:** **babbione** m. crotchety old man, old fart.

**SYNONYM:** **bavoso/a** n. • (lit.): slobbering (from the verb *sbavare*, meaning "to slobber").

**bocciare** v. to crash into someone • (lit.): to knock away the opponent's wooden ball in the game of bocce.

    *example:* La mia nuova macchina è rovinata. Un tipo, passando col rosso, me l'ha **bocciata**!

    *translation:* My new car is ruined. Some guy went through a red light and **bashed into** it!

    **NOTE:** As seen in Lesson One, the verb *bocciare* can also be used to mean "to flunk."

    **SYNONYM -1:** **arrotare** v. • (lit.): to sharpen.

    **SYNONYM -2:** **stendere** v. to hit a pedestrian with a vehicle • (lit.): to spread.

**bomba** f. said of any fantastic possession • (lit.): a bomb.

    *example:* Che **bomba** di macchina hai! Ne ho sempre desiderata una uguale!

    *translation:* What a **great car** you have! I've always wanted one just like it!

    **NOTE:** As seen in Lesson Two, the noun *bomba* can also be used to mean "a blast (of fun)."

**carcassa** f. ramshackle car • (lit.): carcass.

    *example:* Mi piace la tua macchina nuova! Che fine ha fatto la tua vecchia **carcassa**?

    *translation:* I love your new car! What did you do with your old **carcass**?

    **SYNONYM -1:** **bagnarola** f. (Northern & Central Italy) • (lit.): from the popular French slang term for car: *bagnole*.

    **SYNONYM -2:** **carretta** f. • (lit.): two-wheeled cart, wheelbarrow.

    **SYNONYM -3:** **catorcio** m. • (lit.): old thing in bad shape.

**culo (avere un gran)** exp. to be very lucky • (lit.): to have a big ass.

    *example:* Alberto si è rotto il collo, ma ha anche **avuto un gran culo**, perchè si tratta soltanto di una lieve frattura.

*translation:* Alberto broke his neck but was **very lucky**. It was only a minor fracture.

**NOTE -1:** Although this expression uses the masculine noun *culo,* literally meaning "ass," its connotation is <u>not</u> as strong as in English. It is important to remember that by European standards, Americans are considered somewhat prudish and many terms that would be considered highly offensive in the United States are quite acceptable in other countries such as Italy.

**NOTE -2:** You may have noticed that in the dialogue, the adjective *bel* was used in the expression: *"Ho avuto un <u>bel</u> culo…"* This is an extremely popular usage of *bel/bella,* used to mean: **1.** a real…; • **2.** smack dab. For example: **1.** *Gino è un bell'idiota!;* Gino is a real idiot! • **2.** *nel bel mezzo della notte;* smack dab in the middle of the night.

**VARIATION:** **avere un culo bestiale** *exp.* to be extremely lucky • (lit.): to have beastly luck (ass).

**SYNONYM:** **avere fondello** *exp.* (Central Italy) • (lit.): to have bottom.

**kaput** *adj.* (from German) broken, "kaput."

*example:* Il mio computer è **kaput**. Dovrò comprarmene uno nuovo quando avrò un po'di soldi.

*translation:* My computer is **kaput**. I'm going to have to buy a new one as soon as I have the money.

**Occhio!** *interj.* Watch out! Keep your eyes peeled! • (lit.): Eye!

*example:* **Occhio**! Va'piano per queste scale perchè sono molto ripide.

*translation:* **Watch out**! Walk carefully because these steps are very steep.

**pula (la)** *f.* the police, the "cops" • (lit.): husk.

*example:* Da grande Nicola vuole entrare nella **pula**.

*translation:* When Nicholas grows up, he wants to be a **cop**.

**SYNONYM -1:** **piedipiatti** *m.* • (lit.): flat feet.

**NOTE:** It's interesting to note that the American equivalent, *flatfoot,* was an old slang term for "cop."

**SYNONYM -2:** **sbirro** *m.* • (lit.): from Latin *birrum,* meaning "hooded cloak."

**scheggiare** *v.* to drive very fast • (lit.): to splinter.

> *example:* La mia macchina nuova è di grossa cilindrata. Non ti puoi nemmeno immaginare quanto **scheggi**!
>
> *translation:* My new car has a lot of power. You won't believe how it can **haul**!

**sgommare** *f.* (said of a car) to peel out with the scretching of tires • (lit.): to make tires or "to make tracks."

> *example:* Non appena è scattato il verde, Marco è partito **sgommando** con la sua Ferrari nuova di zecca.
>
> *translation:* As soon as the light turned green, Marco **peeled out** in his brand new Ferrari.
>
> **NOTE:** **gomma** *f.* tire.

**spappolare** *v.* to kill• (lit.): to crush or crumble.

> *example:* Mentre attraversavo la strada, un autista è passato col rosso e per poco non mi **spappolava**!
>
> *translation:* As I was walking across the street, a driver ran the red light and almost **killed** me!

**spaziale** *adj.* awesome, fantastic • (lit.): spacial.

> *example:* Che bel vestito! È davvero **spaziale**!
>
> *translation:* What a great dress! It's **awesome**!
>
> **SYNONYM -1:** **boreale** *adj.* (Northern Italy) • (lit.): borealis.
>
> **SYNONYM -2:** **cosmico** *adj.* • (lit.): cosmic.
>
> > **NOTE:** It's interesting to note that in the 1970s, *cosmic* was a popular term in the United States, meaning "fantastic."
>
> **SYNONYM -3:** **fine del mondo** *exp.* • (lit.): the end of the world.
>
> **SYNONYM -4:** **da flash** *exp.* (from English) • (lit.): from a flash or bulletin (such as a "newsflash").
>
> **SYNONYM -5:** **galattico** *adj.* • (lit.): galactic.
>
> **SYNONYM -6:** **il massimo/la massima** *adj.* • (lit.): the maximum.
>
> **SYNONYM -7:** **mitico/a** *adj.* • (lit.): mythical, of mythic proportion.
>
> **SYNONYM -8:** **mostruoso/a** *adj.* • (lit.): monstrous.

**SYNONYM -9:**   **pazzesco/a** *adj.* (Northern & Central Italy) • (lit.): crazy, insane.

**SYNONYM -10:**   **sano/a** *adj.* • (lit.): sane • It's interesting that in English, the opposite in slang applies: *What an <u>insane</u> car!*

**SYNONYM -11:**   **tosto/a** *adj.* • (lit.): toasted.

**SYNONYM -12:**   **troppo** *adj.* • (lit.): too much.

**spennare** *v.* to swindle, to fleece • (lit.): to pluck.

    *example:*   Ho mangiato in un ristorante caro, dove mi hanno **spennato**!

    *translation:*   I ate in an expensive restaurant where I got **fleeced**!

**VARIATION:**   **spennato/a** *adj.* broke • (lit.): unfeathered.

**stoppare** *v.* (from English, most commonly used in soccer) to stop.

    *example -1:*   Ronaldo ha **stoppato** il pallone, ha calciato, e ha segnato un bel goal.

    *translation:*   Ronaldo **stopped** the ball, kicked it, and scored a beautiful goal.

    *example -2:*   **Stoppa**! Hai quasi arrotato un pedone. Fa' attenzione!

    *translation:*   **Stop**! You almost ran over that pedestrian. Be careful!

**strappo** *m.* a ride, a lift • (lit.): a tear.

    *example:*   Vuoi che ti dia uno **strappo** al mercato?

    *translation:*   Would you like me to give you a **lift** to the market?

**succhiare** *v.* (said of a car) to guzzle gas • (lit.): to suck.

    *example:*   Hai finito di nuovo la benzina? Non ho mai visto una macchina che **succhia** quanto la tua!

    *translation:*   You ran out of gas again? I've never seen a car that **guzzles** the way yours does!

**SYNONYM -1:**   **bere** *v.* • (lit.): to drink.

    **ALSO:**   **Questa non la bevo!** *exp.* I don't believe that! • (lit.): I'm not drinking (swallowing) that!

**SYNONYM -2:**   **poppare** *v.* • (lit.): to suck (from the feminine noun *poppa*, meaning "breast").

# PRACTICE THE VOCABULARY

*(Answers to Lesson Three, p. 178)*

## A. Fill in the blanks with the word that best completes the phrase.

| | |
|---|---|
| **BOMBA** | **SPAPPOLAVA** |
| **CARCASSA** | **SPAZIALE** |
| **FRESCO** | **SPENNATO** |
| **SASSATE** | **STRAPPO** |
| **SCHEGGI** | **SUCCHIA** |

1. Che _____ di macchina hai! Ne ho sempre desiderata una uguale!

2. Mentre attraversavo la strada, un automobilista è passato col rosso e per poco non mi _____!

3. Non riesco a credere come la gente guidi in questa città. Vanno tutti come le _____!

4. Vuoi che ti dia uno _____ al mercato?

5. Che bel vestito! È davvero _____!

6. La mia macchina nuova è di grossa cilindrata. Non ti puoi nemmeno immaginare come _____!

7. Mi piace la tua macchina nuova! Che fine ha fatto la tua vecchia _____?

8. Ho mangiato in un ristorante caro, dove mi hanno _____!

9. Hai finito di nuovo la benzina? Non ho mai visto una macchina che _____ quanto la tua!

10. Il rapinatore passerà cinque anni al _____.

## B. Match the English phrase in the left column with the Italian translation in the right. Write the appropriate letter in the box.

☐ 1. Wow! What a beautiful rainbow!

☐ 2. My new teacher is an old geezer. She must be a hundred years old!

☐ 3. My mechanic fleeced me! The repairs on my car cost a fortune!

☐ 4. This is the third time I've been to the gas station. My new car really guzzles gas.

☐ 5. I need to buy a new television. Mine is on the blink.

☐ 6. Watch out! There are a lot of potholes in this street.

☐ 7. When are you going to buy yourself a new car? You've had that ramshackle car for years!

☐ 8. I'm lost. I'm going to ask that cop for directions.

☐ 9. Would you like me to give you a lift to the market?

☐ 10. Everyone really drives fast in this city!

A. Questa è la terza volta che mi fermo dal benzinaio. La mia nuova macchina **succhia** tantissimo.

B. Quando è che ti comprerai una nuova macchina? Sono anni che hai questa **carcassa**!

C. La mia nuova insegnante è una vecchia **babbiona**. Deve avere cent'anni!

D. Mi sono perso. Chiederò indicazioni alla **pula**.

E. Devo comparmi una televisione nuova. Quella che ho ora è **kaput**.

F. Il mio meccanico mi ha **spennato**! Le riparazioni della mia auto mi sono costate una fortuna!

G. Occhio! Ci sono un sacco di buche per strada.

H. Vuoi che ti dia uno **strappo** al mercato?

I. **Ammazza**! Che splendido arcobaleno!

J. Tutti vanno davvero **come le sassate** in questa città!

## C. CROSSWORD
**Fill in the crossword puzzle on page 52 by choosing the appropriate word from the list below.**

| | | |
|---|---|---|
| AMMAZZA | KAPUT | SPAPPOLARE |
| BABBIONA | OCCHIO | SPAZIALE |
| BOCCIARE | PULA | SPENNARE |
| BOMBA | SASSATE | STOPPARE |
| CARCASSA | SCHEGGIARE | STRAPPO |
| CULO | SGOMMARE | SUCCHIARE |

## ACROSS

1. _____ v. to drive very fast • (lit.): to splinter.

18. _____ v. to go broke • (lit.): to lose one's feathers (from *penna*, meaning "feather").

23. _____! *interj*. Watch out! Keep your eyes peeled!

28. _____ f. crotchety old woman, old geezer.

45. _____ adj. awesome, fantastic.

52. _____ m. a ride, a lift • (lit.): a tear.

59. _____ adj. (from German) broken.

61. _____ **(avere un gran)** *exp*. to be very lucky • (lit.): to have a big ass.

## DOWN

1. _____ *v.* to kill • (lit.): to crush or crumble.

8. _____**!** *interj.* Wow! • (lit.): from the verb *ammazzare*, meaning "to kill" – therefore the closest literal translation could be "Killer!"

18. _____ *v.* to guzzle gas (said of a car) • (lit.): to suck.

22. _____ *f.* (said of a car) to peel out with the scretching of tires • (lit.): to make tires or "to make tracks."

26. _____ *f.* ramshackle car.

28. _____ *f.* said of any fantastic possession.

29. _____ *v.* to crash into someone • (lit.): to knock away the opponent's wood in the game of bocce.

34. _____ *v.* (from English, most commonly used in soccer) to stop.

43. **andare come le** _____ *exp.* to be extremely fast, to go as fast as a rocket• (lit.): to go like thrown rocks or projectiles.

54. _____ **(la)** *f.* the police, the "cops" • (lit.): husk.

# CROSSWORD PUZZLE

# D. Underline the word that best completes the phrase.

1. Devo comprarmi un nuovo computer. Quello che ho ora è completamente (**casino**, **kaput**, **occhio**).

2. (**Azzanna**, **Amara**, **Ammazza**)! Hai visto quel fulmine?

3. Ho appena speso tutti i miei soldi per comprarmi un paio di scarpe. Penso che mi abbiano (**appannato**, **spennato**, **affettato**).

4. Hai intenzione di andare a piedi fino all'aeroporto? Mi farebbe piacere darti uno (**strappo**, **tappo**, **straccio**)!

5. Credo che quell'uomo stia rapinando la banca! Svelto! Va' a chiamare la (**pala**, **pula**, **mula**)!

6. Sei appena stato promosso?! (**Spaziale**, **Speziale**, **Iniziale**)!

7. La mia nuova vicina di casa è una vecchia (**pallona**, **barbona**, **babbiona**). Deve aver superato i cent'anni.

8. Patrizia ha vinto alla lotteria per la seconda volta! Ha davvero un gran (**callo**, **culo**, **pulo**)!

9. Sta' attento! Sei quasi passato con il rosso! Vuoi che tu ed io finiamo (**spappolati**, **popolati**, **spennati**)?!

10. La mia nuova macchina può davvero (**scheggiare**, **schiacciare**, **schedare**)! Devo stare attento a non beccarmi una multa.

## E. DICTATION
## Test Your Listening Comprehension

*(This dictation can be found in the Appendix on page 194.)*

If you are following along with your cassette, you will now hear a series of sentences from the opening dialogue. These sentences will be read by a native speaker at normal conversational speed (which may seem fast to you at first). In addition, the words will be pronounced as you would actually hear them in a conversation, often including some common reductions.

The first time the sentences are presented, simply listen in order to get accustomed to the speed and heavy use of reductions. The sentences will then be read again with a pause after each to give you time to write down what you heard. The third time the sentences are read, follow along with what you have written.

# Il mio ospite comincia a *starmi sull'anima!*

*(trans.): My houseguest is starting to get **on my nerves**!*
*(lit.): My houseguest is starting to get **on my soul**!*

*Franco:*   Ciao, Roberto! Come va? Che succede con il tuo ospite?

*Roberto:*   **Non ne posso più**! Quello è davvero una **fogna**. **Ha sempre una fame da lupo**. **Sgrifa**, poi **si abbiocca** e passa il resto del giorno a letto. Qualche volta **si spara** addirittura un panino o due nel bel mezzo della notte, facendo un **casino** incredibile. C'era un **sacco** di cibo in frigo ieri sera, e stamani un **accidente**.

*Franco:*   Che **faccia tosta**!

*Roberto:*   E puzza **da morire** perchè **si tira** due pachetti di **paglie** al giorno!

*Franco:*   Perchè non gli dici di **levarsi di torno**?

*Roberto:*   Ma come faccio? È il mio fratellino! Lui è una persona molto intelligente, anzi direi una **cima**, ma è anche un gran **burino**. Lo farei stare in albergo, ma è sempre **a corto di** lira.

*Franco:*   Da come ne parli, sembra che ti **stia sull'anima**.

# My houseguest is starting to get *on my nerves!*

*Franco:* Hi Roberto! What's up? How's it going with your houseguest?

*Roberto:* **I can't take it anymore**! The guy's a **bottomless pit**. He's **always hungry**. He **stuffs himself** and then **conks out** early and spends all day in bed. Sometimes he even **powers down** a sandwich or two in the middle of the night, making so much **noise**! There was a **pile** of food in the fridge last night, and this morning there's **zip**!

*Franco:* What **nerve**!

*Roberto:* And he stinks **big-time** because he **smokes** two packs of **cigarettes** a day!

*Franco:* Why don't you just tell him **to beat it**?

*Roberto:* But how? He's my little brother. He's a person of high intelligence and **ability** but he's also a **crude, ill-bred individual**. I'd make him stay in a hotel but he's always **short on** money.

*Franco:* It sounds like he's **getting on your nerves**.

# My houseguest is starting to get *on my soul!*

*Franco:* Hi Roberto! What's up? How's it going with your houseguest?

*Roberto:* **I can't anymore of it**! The guy's a **sewer**. He **always has the hunger of a wolf**. He **snorts** and then **dozes off** early and spends the rest of the day in bed. Sometimes he even **shoots himself** a sandwich or two in the middle of the night, making so much **brothel**! There was a **sack** of food in the fridge last night and this morning there's **zip**!

*Franco:* What **toasted face**!

*Roberto:* And he stinks **to die from** because he **pulls** two packs of **straws** a day!

*Franco:* Why don't you just tell him **to get himself up from around here**?

*Roberto:* But how? He's my little brother. He's a person of high intelligence and a **top** but he's also a **crude, ill-bred individual**. I'd make him stay in a hotel but he's always **short on** money.

*Franco:* It sounds like he's **getting on your soul**.

# VOCABULARY

**a corto di qualcosa (essere)** *exp.* to be short on something • (lit.): to be at short of something.

> *example:* Mi piacerebbe andare al cinema con te, ma questa settimana sono **a corto di** soldi.

> *translation:* I'd like to go with you to the movies, but **I'm short on** money this week.

**abbioccarsi** *v.* to fall asleep, to doze off.

> *example:* Dopo cena Gianni ha bevuto due bicchieri di grappa e **si è abbioccato** subito sul divano.

> *translation:* After dinner Gianni had two glasses of grappa and **dozed off** right away on the couch.

**accidente (un)** *adv.* nothing, "zip," "nada" • (lit.): accident, mishap.

> *example:* Sai cosa mi ha regalato Franco per il mio compleanno? **Un accidente**!

> *translation:* Do you know what Franco gave me for my birthday? **Zip**!

> **SYNONYM -1:** **nisba** *adv.* (Northern & Central Italy) • (lit.): from the German word *nichts,* meaning "nothing."

> **SYNONYM -2:** **ostia** *f.* • (lit.): host.

> **SYNONYM -3:** **un corno** *m.* • (lit.): a horn.

> **SYNONYM -4:** **un kaiser** *m.* • (lit.): a kaiser (from the German word, *Kaiser,* meaning "emperor").

> **SYNONYM -5:** **un tubo** *m.* (Central Italy) • (lit.): a tube.

> **SYNONYM -6:** **una madonna** *f.* • (lit.): a Madonna.

> **SYNONYM -7:** **una mazza** *f.* • (lit.): a sledgehammer.

**burino** *m.* a crude, ill-bred individual.

> *example:* Piero è andato a una cena molto elegante con una giacca bianca e un mazzetto di banconote da cento dollari che gli uscivano dal taschino. Che **burino**!
>
> *translation:* Piero went to a very formal gala dinner wearing a white jacket with a bunch of $100 bills sticking out of his pocket. What a **crude person**!

**casino (fare)** *exp.* to make a lot of noise • (lit.): to make a brothel.

> *example:* I miei vicini hanno avuto una festa ieri sera e hanno **fatto un gran casino**. Non sono riuscito a dormire un minuto!
>
> *translation:* The neighbors had a big party and made **a lot of noise**. I couldn't sleep a minute!
>
> **NOTE:** You'll notice in the dialogue that the indefinite article *"un"* was used before *casino*. Whenever *casino* is modified by an adjective, in this case *incredibile*, *"un"* must precede *casino*.

**cima** *f.* a genius, a "brain" • (lit.): top.

> *example:* Anna ha finito tutti i problemi in meno di dieci minuti! Lei è davvero una **cima**!
>
> *translation:* Anna finished all the problems in less than ten minutes! She is really a **brain**!

**da morire** *adj.* (used to modify a noun or verb) big-time • (lit.): from dying.

> *example:* Questo caffè è buono **da morire**!
>
> *translation:* This coffee is **to die for**!

**faccia tosta** *exp.* nerve, brazenness • (lit.): toasted face.

> *example:* Paolo mi ha dapprima insultato ed offeso durante l'intera conversazione, poi mi ha invitato alla sua festa. Che **faccia tosta** che ha!
>
> *translation:* First Paolo insulted me and swore at me during the whole conversation, then he invited me to his party! What **nerve**!

**fame da lupo (avere una)** *exp.* to be extremely hungry • (lit.): to have a hunger of a wolf.

> *example:* A che ora ceniamo? **Ho una fame da lupo**!
>
> *translation:* What time are we eating dinner? **I'm starving**!

**fogna (essere una)** *f.* to be a bottomless pit, said of someone who will swallow anything literally and metaphorically • (lit.): to be a sewer.

> *example:* Davide ha mangiato tutto quello che c'era nel frigo e ha ancora fame. È proprio una **fogna**!
>
> *translation:* David ate everything in the refrigerator and he's still hungry! What a **bottomless pit**!

> **SYNONYM:** **cloaca** *f.* • (lit.): sewer, drain, cesspool.

**levarsi di torno** *exp.* to leave a place, to "beat it" • (lit.): to get oneself up from around here.

> *example:* **Levati di torno**! Non dovresti essere qui!
>
> *translation:* **Get out of here**! You're not supposed to be here!

> **SYNONYM -1:** **alzare i tacchi** *exp.* to get moving • (lit.): to lift one's heels • *Alza i tacchi!*; Get lost!

> **SYNONYM -2:** **Aria!** *interj.* Get lost! • (lit.): air.

> **SYNONYM -3:** **circolare** *v.* • (lit.): to circulate • (lit.): *Circola!*; Get lost!

> **SYNONYM -4:** **scarpinare** *v.* • (lit.): to move one's shoes • *Scarpina!*; Get lost!

> **SYNONYM -5:** **smammare** *v.* (from Naples) • *Smamma!*; Get lost!

**non poterne più** *exp.* to be unable to take it any longer • (lit.): not to be able of it any longer.

> *example:* **Non ne posso più**! Il capo non mi piace e l'orario è lunghissimo! Domani mattina smetto!
>
> *translation:* **I can't take it any longer**! I don't like my boss and the hours are terribly long. I'm going to quit in the morning!

**paglia** *f.* cigarette • (lit.): straw.

> *example:* Alberto ha soltanto dodici anni e si fa già le **paglie**!
>
> *translation:* Alberto is only twelve years old and he's already smoking **cigarettes**!

**NOTE:** **farsi una paglia** *exp.* to smoke • (lit.): to do oneself a straw.

**SYNONYM -1:** **bionda** *f.* a cigarette made from blond tobacco • (lit.): blond.

**SYNONYM -2:** **cicca** *f.* (Northern & Central Italy) • (lit.): from the French word *chique,* meaning "chewing tobacco."

**sacco** *m.* a lot, a large quantity • (lit.): a sack.

    *example:* Gina ha un **sacco** di soldi. Lei compra una nuova macchina tutti i mesi!

    *translation:* Gina has **a lot** of money. She buys a new car every month!

**SYNONYM -1:** **un casino** *m.* • (lit.): a brothel.

**SYNONYM -2:** **un fracco** *m.* (Northern Italy)

**SYNONYM -3:** **un frego** *m.* (Central Italy) • (lit.): from the verb *fregare,* meaning "to rub" or, in slang, "to swindle."

**SYNONYM -4:** **un macello** *m.* • (lit.): a slaughter.

**sgrifare** *v.* to wolf down food • (lit.): to snort.

    *example:* Hai visto come Roberta ha **sgrifato** tutta quella torta? Che schifo!

    *translation:* Did you see Roberta **wolf down** that entire pie? It was disgusting!

**SYNONYM -1:** **pappare** *v.* • (lit.): from *pappa,* meaning "baby food."

**SYNONYM -2:** **sbafare** *v.* • (lit.): from *sbafo,* meaning "a meal that one eats without paying for it."

**SYNONYM -3:** **spazzolare** *v.* • (lit.): to brush.

**SYNONYM -4:** **strafognarsi** *v.* • (lit.): from *fogna,* meaning "sewer."

**spararsi** *v.* to partake, to treat oneself to something • (lit.): to shoot oneself.

    *example:* Dopo cena **mi sparo** un po' di musica e poi me ne vado a letto.

    *translation:* After dinner, I'm going **to enjoy** a little music and then I'm going to bed.

**sull'anima (stare)** *exp.* to annoy, to get on someone's nerves • (lit.): to be on one's soul.

> *example:* Il nuovo impiegato **mi sta davvero sull'anima**! Non sta mai zitto!
>
> *translation:* The new employee is really **getting on my nerves**! He never shuts up!
>
> **SYNONYM -1:** **stare sui calli a qualcuno** *exp.* • (lit.): to stand on someone's corns.
>
> **SYNONYM -2:** **scassare** *v.* • (lit.): to unpack.
>
> **SYNONYM -3:** **tafanare** *v.* • (lit.): from *tafano*, meaning "horsefly" (insinuating that someone is as annoying as a huge fly).

**tirare** *v.* to smoke • (lit.): to pull (a puff of smoke).

> *example:* Da quanto è che **tiri**? Non sai che ti fa male?
>
> *translation:* How long have you been **smoking**? Don't you know it's bad for your health?
>
> **VARIATION:** **fare un tiro** *exp.* to take a puff of a cigarette • (lit.): to make a pull.

# PRACTICE THE VOCABULARY

*(Answers to Lesson Four, p. 180)*

## A. Choose the letter which corresponds to the correct definition of the words in boldface.

1. **abbioccarsi**:
   a. to fall asleep
   b. to drink in excess

2. **un accidente**:
   a. a lot
   b. nothing, "zip"

3. **fogna (essere una)**:
   a. to smell bad
   b. to be a bottomless pit, said of someone who eats nonstop

4. **paglia**:
   a. cigarette
   b. a very thin person

5. **casino (fare)**:
   a. to gamble excessively
   b. to make a lot of noise

6. **faccia tosta**:
   a. nerve, brazenness
   b. red face due to alcohol

7. **sacco**:
   a. a lot, a large quantity
   b. a job that is difficult to perform

8. **sgrifare**:
   a. to wolf down food
   b. to leave quickly

9. **sull'anima (stare)**:
   a. to annoy
   b. to sleep

10. **tirare**:
    a. to smoke
    b. to fall

11. **levarsi di torno**:
    a. to be a bottomless pit, to eat nonstop
    b. to leave a place, to "beat it"

12. **non poterne più**:
    a. to have insomnia
    b. to be unable to take it any longer

## B. FIND-A-WORD PUZZLE
**Using the list below, circle the words in the grid on page 67 that are missing from the definition below. The words may be spelled vertically or horizontally.**

| | |
|---|---|
| **ABBIOCCARSI** | **MORIRE** |
| **ACCIDENTE** | **PAGLIA** |
| **ANIMA** | **PIÙ** |
| **BURINO** | **SACCO** |
| **CASINO** | **SGRIFARE** |
| **CIMA** | **SPARARSI** |
| **CORTO** | **TIRARE** |
| **FOGNA** | **TORNO** |
| **LUPO** | **TOSTA** |

1. **a ____ di qualcosa (essere)** *exp.* to be short on something • (lit.): to be at short of something.

2. **____ (fare)** *exp.* to make a lot of noise • (lit.): to make a brothel.

3. **da ____** *adj.* (used to modify a noun or verb) big-time • (lit.): from dying.

4. **fame da ____ (avere una)** *exp.* to be extremely hungry • (lit.): to have the hunger of a wolf.

5. **____ (essere una)** *f.* to be a bottomless pit, said of someone who will swallow anything literally and metaphorically • (lit.): to be a sewer.

6. **non poterne ____** *exp.* to be unable to take it any longer • (lit.): not to be able any longer.

7.  \_\_\_\_ *m.* a lot, a large quantity.

8.  \_\_\_\_ **(un)** *adv.* nothing, "zip," "nada" • (lit.): accident, mishap.

9.  \_\_\_\_ *f.* cigarette • (lit.): straw.

10. \_\_\_\_ *v.* to partake, to treat oneself to something • (lit.): to shoot oneself.

11. \_\_\_\_ *v.* to smoke • (lit.): to pull (a puff of smoke).

12. **sull'**\_\_\_\_ **(stare)** *exp.* to annoy, to get on someone's nerves • (lit.): to be on one's soul.

13. \_\_\_\_ *v.* to wolf down food • (lit.): to snort.

14. **levarsi di** \_\_\_\_ *exp.* to leave a place, to "beat it" • (lit.): to get oneself up from around here.

15. \_\_\_\_ *v.* to falls asleep, to doze off.

16. \_\_\_\_ *f.* a genius, a "brain" • (lit.): top.

17. **faccia** \_\_\_\_ *exp.* nerve, brazenness • (lit.): toasted face.

18. \_\_\_\_ *m.* someone with little or no class, tacky person.

# FIND-A-WORD PUZZLE

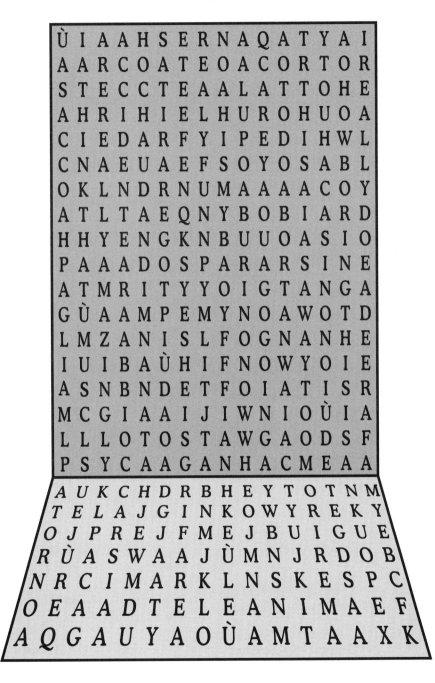

Ù I A A H S E R N A Q A T Y A I
A A R C O A T E O A C O R T O R
S T E C C T E A A L A T T O H E
A H R I H I E L H U R O H U O A
C I E D A R F Y I P E D I H W L
C N A E U A E F S O Y O S A B L
O K L N D R N U M A A A A C O Y
A T L T A E Q N Y B O B I A R D
H H Y E N G K N B U U O A S I O
P A A A D O S P A R A R S I N E
A T M R I T Y Y O I G T A N G A
G Ù A A M P E M Y N O A W O T D
L M Z A N I S L F O G N A N H E
I U I B A Ù H I F N O W Y O I E
A S N B N D E T F O I A T I S R
M C G I A A I J I W N I O Ù I A
L L L O T O S T A W G A O D S F
P S Y C A A G A N H A C M E A A
A U K C H D R B H E Y T O T N M
T E L A J G I N K O W Y R E K Y
O J P R E J F M E J B U I G U E
R Ù A S W A A J Ù M N J R D O B
N R C I M A R K L N S K E S P C
O E A A D T E L E A N I M A E F
A Q G A U Y A O Ù A M T A A X K

## C. Match the English phrase in the left column with the Italian translation in the right. Write the appropriate letter in the box.

☐ 1. Gina has **a lot** of money. She buys a new car every month!

☐ 2. After dinner, I'm going **to enjoy** a little music and then I'm going to bed.

☐ 3. This coffee is **to die for**!

☐ 4. Piero went to a very formal gala dinner wearing a white jacket with a bunch of $100 bills sticking out of his pocket. What a **crude person**!

☐ 5. Do you know what Franco gave me for my birthday? **Zip**!

☐ 6. I'd like to go with you to the movies, but **I'm short on** money this week.

☐ 7. How long have you been **smoking**? Don't you know it's bad for your health?

☐ 8. Anna finished all the problems in less than ten minutes! She is really a **brain**!

☐ 9. What time are we eating dinner? **I'm starving**!

☐ 10. The new employee is really **getting on my nerves**! He never shuts up!

A. Mi piacerebbe andare al cinema con te, ma questa settimana sono **a corto di** soldi.

B. Anna ha finito tutti i problemi in meno di dieci minuti! Lei è davvero una **cima**!

C. Gina ha un **sacco** di soldi. Lei compra una nuova maccina tutti i mesi.

D. Il nuovo impiegato **mi sta davvero sull'anima**! Non sta mai zitto!

E. Piero è andato a una cena molto elegante con una giacca bianca e un mazzetto di banconote da cento dollari che gli uscivano dal taschino. Che **burino**!

F. Dopo cena, **mi sparo** un po'di musica e poi me ne vado a letto.

G. Sai cosa mi ha regalato Franco per il mio compleanno? **Un accidente**!

H. Questo caffè è buono **da morire**!

I. Da quanto è che **tiri**? Non sai che ti fa male?

J. A che ora ceniamo? **Ho una fame da lupo**!

# D. Fill in the following blanks with the letter that corresponds to the best answer.

1. La commedia era così noiosa che ____ per quasi tutto il tempo!
   a. mi sono svegliato
   b. mi sono ubriacato
   c. mi sono abbioccato

2. Marcello farebbe meglio a stare attento.  Se non smette di ____ finirà in ospedale!
   a. atterrare
   b. tirare
   c. attirare

3. Levati di ____! Non sei abbastanza grande per stare qui!
   a. torno
   b. forno
   c. contorno

4. Hai visto quanto ha mangiato Lorenzo alla festa? È proprio una ____!
   a. fogna
   b. pigna
   c. lagna

5. Sono a ____ di soldi.  Me ne puoi prestare un po'?
   a. carta
   b. lordo
   c. corto

6. Sai cosa mi ha regalato Franco per il mio compleanno? Un ____!
   a. incidente
   b. accidente
   c. dente

7. Non sono riuscito a dormire un minuto! I miei vicini hanno avuto una festa ieri sera e hanno fatto un gran _____.
   a. abbaino
   b. cantina
   c. casino

8. Tuo fratello ha inventato una macchina che non va a benzina! Deve essere davvero una ____.
   a. cima
   b. ciospa
   c. lima

9. Che torta deliziosa! È buona ____!
   a. da morire
   b. da soffrire
   c. da patire

10. Non ho mangiato niente dalla prima colazione. Ho una fame da ____!
    a. pula
    b. lupo
    c. lume

11. Sono stanco di fare tutti questi compiti. Non ne posso ____!
    a. poi
    b. però
    c. più

12. È la decima ____ che fumi in un'ora. Non credi che dovresti smettere per un po'?
    a. maglia
    b. paglia
    c. foglia

13. Hai visto come Roberta ha ____ tutta quella torta? Che schifo!
    a. schifato
    b. ghignato
    c. sgrifato

14. Il mio nuovo vicino di casa mi sta proprio sull'____. Ogni volta che mi vede, la mattina, comincia a parlarmi senza mai fermarsi e io non riesco a liberarmi di lui.
    a. ascella
    b. anima
    c. asina

# E. DICTATION
## Test Your Listening Comprehension

*(This dictation can be found in the Appendix on page 194.)*

If you are following along with your cassette, you will now hear a series of sentences from the opening dialogue. These sentences will be read by a native speaker at normal conversational speed (which may seem fast to you at first). In addition, the words will be pronounced as you would actually hear them in a conversation, often including some common reductions.

The first time the sentences are presented, simply listen in order to get accustomed to the speed and heavy use of reductions. The sentences will then be read again with a pause after each to give you time to write down what you heard. The third time the sentences are read, follow along with what you have written.

# Come fa uno a vivere in una tale *topaia*?

*(trans.): How can anyone live in such a* **rattrap**?
*(lit.): How can anyone live in such a* **mouse hole**?

# LEZIONE CINQUE · Dialogue in Slang

Alessandra:   Ciao, Alberto e Chiara!  Vi state divertendo al mio **party**?

Alberto:   Oh, sì! **Alla grande**!  È una gran **figata**!

   *[Poi, quando Alessandra si allontana…]*

   **Che palle**! Stento a credere che lei riesca a vivere in questa **topaia**! Ascolta, **ho fatto il pieno**! **Filiamocela**!

Chiara:   Siamo appena arrivati!  Oh, no.  Vedi quel **buzzino** con quel paio di vecchie **barche** ai piedi?  Si chiama Roberto Ferri. Spero che non mi veda!  Lui mi **sta davvero sul culo**. Quello **stronzo ci prova** tutte le volte con me.  Continuo a **mandarlo al diavolo** ma quella **testa di rapa** non demorde e insiste a voler uscire con me.  Ti assicuro che se è per me lui continuerà ad **andare in bianco**. Chi è quella **ciospa** con quei **trampoli** che gli sta vicino?

Alberto:   Oh, quella è Annamaria Corsi.  Lei è diventata davvero una **balena**!

Chiara:   Non mi sorprende. Guarda come **si abbuffa come un maiale**!

# How can anyone live in such a rattrap?

*Alessandra:* Hi Alessio and Chiara! Are you having fun at my **party**?

*Alberto:* Oh, yes! **Big time**! What a **blast**!

*[Then as Alessandra walks away…]*

**What a bore**! I can't believe she lives in such a **rattrap**! **I've had enough**. Let's **get out of here**!

*Chiara:* We just got here! Oh no. See that **fatso** over there wearing the ugly old **shoes**? That's Roberto Ferri. I hope he doesn't see me. He **really bugs me**. That **jerk** keeps **trying to hit on me** all the time. I keep telling him **to get lost** but that **nerd** keeps bothering me. I can assure you that he's **not going to get anywhere**. Who's the **scarecrow** with the **high heels** he's standing next to?

*Alberto:* Oh, that's Annamaria Corsi. She's turned into such a **blimp**.

*Chiara:* I'm not surprised. Look at the way she's **stuffing her face**!

# How can anyone live in such a *mouse hole?*

| | |
|---|---|
| *Alessandra:* | Hi Alessio and Chiara! Are you having a good time at my **party**? |
| *Alberto:* | Oh, yes! **To the big**! What an **extremely positive situation**! |

*[Then as Alessandra walks away…]*

**What balls**! I can't believe she lives in such a **mouse hole**. **I've made the full**. Let's **spin ourselves from it**.

| | |
|---|---|
| *Chiara:* | We just got here! Oh no. See that **belly** over there wearing the ugly old **boats**? That's Roberto Ferri. I hope he doesn't see me. He really stays **on my ass**. That **turd tries himself** with me all the time. I keep **sending him to the devil** but that **beet head** keeps bothering me. I can assure you that he's **going to go in white**. Who's the **troll** with the **stilts** he's standing next to? |
| *Alberto:* | That's Annamaria Corsi. She's turned into such a **whale**. |
| *Chiara:* | I'm not surprised. Look at the way she's **stuffing herself like a pig**. |

# VOCABULARY

**abbuffarsi come un maiale** *exp.* to stuff oneself like a pig.

>   *example:* **Mi sono abbuffato come un maiale** alla festa,
>             e ora mi sento male!
>
>   *translation:* I **ate like a pig** at the party, and now I feel sick!

**alla grande** *adj.* beautifully, big-time • (lit.): to the big.

>   *example:* – Sai se Mario ha passato l'esame?
>             – Sì, lo ha passato **alla grande**!
>
>   *translation:* – Do you know if Mario passed his exam?
>             – Yes, he passed it **beautifully**!

**andare in bianco** *exp.* not to get anywhere romantically with another
person, not to "score" • (lit.): to go in white.

>   *example:* – Come è andata la tua uscita con Alessandra?
>             – **In bianco**! Io non sono affatto il suo tipo!
>
>   *translation:* – How was your date with Alessandra?
>             – **I didn't get anywhere**. I'm not her type at all.

**balena** *f.* fat woman, "blimp" • (lit.): whale.

> *example:*  Che è successo a Roberta? Prima era magrissima e ora è una **balena**!
>
> *translation:*  What happened to Roberta? She used to be so thin and now she's a **blimp**!
>
> **VARIATION:**  **balenottera** *f.*

**barche** *f.pl.* old, worn-out shoes • (lit.): boats.

> *example:*  Quando butterai via quelle **barche** e ti comprerai un paio di scarpe nuove?
>
> *translation:*  When are you going to throw away those **old, worn-out shoes** and get some new ones?

**buzzino** *m.* short, fat man with a potbelly • (lit.): from *buzza,* meaning "belly."

> *example:*  Se continui a bere birra, diventerai un **buzzino**!
>
> *translation:*  If you keep drinking beer all the time, you're going to turn into a **short, fat guy with a potbelly**!

**Che palle!** *inter.* What a drag! • (lit.): What balls!

> *example:*  Le feste di Annamaria sono sempre le peggiori! **Che palle**! Andiamocene!
>
> *translation:*  Annamaria always has the worst parties. **What a drag**! Let's get out of here!
>
> **VARIATION:**  **Che palloso/a!** *interj.*
>
> **SYNONYM -1:**  **Che coma!** *interj.* • (lit.): What a coma!
>
> **SYNONYM -2:**  **Che depressione!** *interj.* • (lit.): What a depression!
>
> **SYNONYM -3:**  **Che mattone!** *interj.* • (lit.): What a brick!
>
> **SYNONYM -4:**  **Che peso/a!** *interj.* (Northern & Central Italy) • (lit.): What heaviness.
>
> **SYNONYM -4:**  **Che pizza!** *interj.* • (lit.): What a pizza!
>
> **SYNONYM -5:**  **Che rottura!** *interj.* • (lit.): What a breaking! (from the verb *rompere,* meaning "to break").

**ciospo/a** *n.* ugly person, "troll."

> *example:* Hai visto Paola? È diventata una **ciospa**!
>
> *translation:* Did you see Paola? She has turned into an **ugly troll**!

**SYNONYM -1:** **racchio/a** *adj.*

**SYNONYM -2:** **scorfano/a** *n.* • (lit.): scorpion fish.


**culo a qualcuno (stare sul)** *exp.* to bug someone big-time • (lit.): to be on someone's ass.

> *example:* Il fratellino di Franco **mi sta davvero sul culo**. Mi segue dappertutto!
>
> *translation:* Franco's little brother really **bugs me**. He follows me everywhere!

**NOTE:** As mentioned earlier, although this expression uses the masculine noun *culo*, literally meaning "ass," its connotation is <u>not</u> as strong as in English. It's important to remember that by European standards, Americans are considered somewhat prudish and many terms that would be considered highly offensive in the United States are quite acceptable in other countries such as Italy.


**fare il pieno** *exp.* to have had all one can tolerate • (lit.): to make the full (commonly used in reference to filling a car's gas tank).

> *example:* **Ho fatto il pieno**! Tutte le volte che vado da Ana, lei mi vuol far sapere quanti soldi ha. È davvero offensivo!
>
> *translation:* **I've had it**! Everytime I go to Ana's house, she brags about how much money she has. It's really offensive!


**figata** *f.* an extremely positive situation or thing, a very "cool" thing.

> *example:* – Ti è piaciuta la festa di Salvatore?
> – Sì! È stata una vera **figata**!
>
> *translation:* – Did you like Salvatore's party?
> – Yes! It was a **blast**!

**SYNONYM -1:** **bomba** *f.* • (lit.): bomb.

**SYNONYM -2:** **cannonata** *f.* • (lit.): cannon shot.

**filarsela** v. to leave quickly, to scram• (lit.): to spin oneself to it.

> *example:* Suona l'allarme! **Filiamocela** prima che la polizia ci veda!
>
> *translation:* The alarm went off! **Let's scram** before the cops see us!

> **SYNONYM -1:** **alzare le fette** exp. • (lit.): to lift one's feet.

> **SYNONYM -2:** **battersela** v. • (lit.): to beat oneself it.

> **SYNONYM -3:** **darsela** v. • (lit.): to give oneself it.

> > **ALSO:** **darsela a gambe** exp. to run away quickly • to give it to oneself to the legs.

> **SYNONYM -4:** **schizzare** v. • (lit.): to squirt.

**mandare qualcuno al diavolo** exp. to tell someone to get lost • (lit.): to send someone to the devil.

> *example:* C'è Roberto. Lui è così fastidioso. Se viene da me, lo **mando al diavolo**!
>
> *translation:* There's Roberto. He's so annoying. If he comes up to me, I'm going to tell him **to get lost**!

> **SYNONYM -1:** **Aria!** interj. Get lost! • (lit.): air.

> **SYNONYM -2:** **mandare qualcuno a quel paese** exp. • (lit.): to send someone to that country.

> **SYNONYM -3:** **mandare qualcuno a fare un bagno** exp. • (lit.): to send someone to take a bath.

> **SYNONYM -4:** **Smamma!** interj. (from the verb *smammare,* meaning "to beat it") Get lost!

**party** m. (borrowed from English) party.

> *example:* – Tutti, tranne me, sono stati invitati al **party** di Alessandra!
> – Forse il tuo invito è andato perduto nella posta.
>
> *translation:* – Everyone, but me, was invited to Alessandra's **party**!
> – Maybe your invitation got lost in the mail.

**provarci** v. to flirt, to hit on someone • (lit.): from the verb *provare,* meaning "to try."

     *example:*  Paolo non **ci prova** più con me, perchè l'ultima volta che l'ha fatto, l'ho mandato al diavolo!

    *translation:*  Paolo doesn't **hit on me** anymore, because the last time he did, I told him to get lost!

**stronzo** *m.* despicable person, jerk • (lit.): turd.

     *example:*  Quello **stronzo** ha appena rotto la mia finestra con un sasso!

    *translation:*  That **jerk** just broke my window with a rock!

    | **SYNONYM -1:** | **cretino/a** *n.* • (lit.): cretin. |

    **SYNONYM -2:**  **fesso/a** *n.* jerk, dimwit, dolt, fool • (lit.): from the verb *fendere*, meaning "to split" – a rough translation could be "someone who is split in the head" or "someone who has half a brain."

    **VARIATION:**  **stronzetto** *m.* (diminutive form of *stronzo*) little jerk.

**testa di rapa** *exp.* nerd, geek, jerk • (lit.): beet head.

     *example:*  Hai visto il tipo con cui Angela è uscita ieri sera? Angela ha detto che si è sporcato tre volte durante la cena. Che **testa di rapa**!

    *translation:*  Did you see the guy Angela went out with last night? Angela said that he got stuff on himself three times during dinner! What a **nerd**!

**topaia** *f.* horrible dwelling, "rattrap" • (lit.): small mouse hole (from the masculine noun *topo*, meaning "mouse").

     *example:*  Giovanni sta spendendo una fortuna per il suo nuovo appartamento, che è soltanto una **topaia**!

    *translation:*  Giovanni is paying a fortune for his new apartment, which is really a **dump**!

**trampoli** *m.pl.* high heels • (lit.): stilts.

     *example:*  Hai visto che **trampoli** portava Giovanna oggi? Sembrava un gigante!

    *translation:*  Did you see the **high heels** Giovanna was wearing today? She looked like a giant!

    **NOTE:**  **Trompoli** is also used to mean "long and thin legs."

# PRACTICE THE VOCABULARY

*(Answers to Lesson Five, p. 181)*

## A. Fill in the blanks with the word that best completes the phrase.

| | |
|---|---|
| BALENA | GRANDE |
| BARCHE | MAIALE |
| BUZZINO | PALLE |
| CIOSPA | TOPAIA |
| FILIAMOCELA | TRAMPOLI |

1. Devo accompagnare mia zia all'aeroporto alle sei di mattina!
   Che_____

2. Raffaele ha mangiato come un _____alla mia festa.  Deve
   avere un bell'appetito!

3. – Vi siete divertiti/e al parco?
   – Certo, alla _____! Abbiamo conosciuto della gente
   molto carina.

4. Hai visto i _____che Giulia portava oggi?  Come fa a
   camminarci?

5. Non puoi metterti quelle vecchie_____per andare al
   ristorante.  Devi assolutamente comprarti un nuovo paio di scarpe.

6. _____! Se non ce ne andiamo ora, arriveranno
   i poliziotti!

7. Come fa Patrizia a vivere in questa _____?
   È così` sporca e schifosa!

8. Vedi quel _____là?  Non è Fabrizio?  Prima era così in
   buona forma e muscoloso.  È davvero cambiato!

9. Sandra mi ha appena detto che si farà un lifting.  Sinceramente
   non credo che niente potrà far migliorare quella

   _____.

10. Se continui a mangiare così, diventerai una _____.

# B. Underline the word that best completes the phrase.

1. Avresti dovuto vedere quella testa di (**rana**, **rapa**, **lana**) con cui Arianna è uscita ieri!

2. Quella (**ciospa**, **cispa**, **cialda**) pensa di poter vincere il concorso di bellezza? Deve essere matta!

3. La festa di Alessandra era orribile. Che (**selle**, **padelle**, **palle**)!

4. Come fai a camminare con quei (**trappole**, **trampoli**, **poli**) senza cadere?

5. Hai invitato Giuliano alla tua festa? Non sopporto quello (**stronzo**, **stretto**, **strano**)!

6. Mi sono divertito moltissimo ieri sera. Che (**pedata**, **fessata**, **figata**)!

7. Ho fatto il (**pieno**, **panno**, **piano**) dei suoi insulti. Me ne vado!

8. Franco mi sta davvero sul (**culo**, **cielo**, **callo**) perchè mi segue dappertutto.

9. Angelo prima era muscolosissimo. Ora è un (**buzzino**, **bazzino**, **bustino**).

10. Guarda come Filippo si abbuffa come un (**portale**, **maiale**, **mistrale**).

11. Se non smette di darmi fastidio, lo mando al (**cavolo**, **pendolo**, **diavolo**).

12. Quelle (**barche**, **bietole**, **brache**) stanno malissimo con i tuoi nuovi pantaloni. Perchè non vai a comprarti delle scarpe nuove?

## C. Match the English phrase in the left column with the Italian translation from the right. Write the appropriate letter in the box.

☐ 1. **I've had it**! Everytime I go to Ana's house, she brags about how much money she has. It's really offensive!

☐ 2. Did you see Paola? She has turned into an **ugly troll**!

☐ 3. Did you see the **high heels** Giovanna was wearing today? She looked like a giant!

☐ 4. Everyone, but me, was invited to Alessandra's **party**!

☐ 5. I **ate like a pig** at the party and now I feel sick!

☐ 6. The alarm went off! **Let's scram** before the cops see us!

☐ 7. That **jerk** just throw a rock through my window!

☐ 8. Giovanni is paying a fortune for his new apartment and it's really a **dump**!

☐ 9. When are you going to throw away those **old, worn-out shoes** and get some new ones?

☐ 10. Paolo doesn't **hit on me** anymore, because the last time he did, I told him to get lost!

A. Giovanni sta spendendo una fortuna per il suo nuovo appartamento, che è soltanto una **topaia**!

B. **Ho fatto il pieno**! Tutte le volte che vado da Ana, lei mi vuol far sapere quanti soldi ha. È davvero offensivo!

C. Hai visto Paola? È diventata una **ciospa**!

D. Paolo non **ci prova** più con me, perchè l'ultima volta che l'ha fatto, l'ho mandato al diavolo!

E. **Mi sono abbuffato come un maiale** alla festa, e ora mi sento male!

F. Hai visto che **trampoli** portava Giovanna oggi? Sembrava un gigante!

G. Quello **stronzo** ha appena rotto la mia finestra con un sasso!

H. Quando butterai via quelle **barche** e ti comprerai un paio di scarpe nuove?

I. Tutti, tranne me, sono stati invitati al **party** di Alessandra!

J. Suona l'allarme! **Filiamocela** prima che la polizia ci veda!

## D. Complete the dialogue using the list below.

| | | |
|---|---|---|
| **BALENA** | **FIGATA** | **PIENO** |
| **BARCHE** | **FILIAMOCELA** | **PROVA** |
| **BUZZINO** | **GRANDE** | **RAPA** |
| **CIOSPA** | **MAIALE** | **STRONZO** |
| **CULO** | **PALLE** | **TOPAIA** |
| **DIAVOLO** | **PARTY** | **TRAMPOLI** |

*Alessandra:*  Ciao, Alberto e Chiara!  Vi state divertendo al mio _____?

*Alberto:*  Oh, sì! Alla _____! È una gran _____!

*[Poi, quando Alessandra si allontana…]*

Che _____! Stento a credere che lei riesca a vivere
in questa _____! Ascolta, ho fatto il _____!
_____!

*Chiara:*  Siamo appena arrivati! Oh, no! Vedi quel _____
con quel paio di vecchie _____ ai piedi?  Si
chiama Roberto Ferri.  Spero che non mi veda!  Lui mi sta
davvero sul _____. Quello _____ ci
_____ tutte le volte con me.  Continuo a mandarlo al
_____ ma quel testa di _____ non
demorde e insiste a voler uscire con me.  Ti assicuro che se è
per me lui continuerà ad andare in bianco. Chi è quella
_____con quei _____ che gli sta vicino?

*Alberto:*  Oh, quella è Annamaria Corsi.  Lei è diventata davvero una
_____!

*Chiara:*  Non mi sorprende. Guarda come si abbuffa come un
_____!

# E. DICTATION
## Test Your Listening Comprehension

*(This dictation can be found in the Appendix on page 195.)*

If you are following along with your cassette, you will now hear a series of sentences from the opening dialogue. These sentences will be read by a native speaker at normal conversational speed (which may seem fast to you at first). In addition, the words will be pronounced as you would actually hear them in a conversation, often including some common reductions.

The first time the sentences are presented, simply listen in order to get accustomed to the speed and heavy use of reductions. The sentences will then be read again with a pause after each to give you time to write down what you heard. The third time the sentences are read, follow along with what you have written.

# REVIEW EXAM FOR LESSONS 1-5

*(Answers to Review, p. 183)*

## A. Choose the correct definition of the words in boldface. Circle your answer.

1. **abbioccarsi**:
   a. to fall asleep
   b. to drink to excess

2. **bomba:**
   a. bad movie or play
   b. blast (of fun)

3. **bottega aperta (avere la):**
   a. to keep late hours, to work overtime
   b. to have one's zipper open

4. **Buona notte!**
   a. Good grief!
   b. Leave me alone!

5. **casino (fare)**:
   a. to gamble excessively
   b. to make a lot of noise

6. **cenci:**
   a. ugly clothing
   b. old car, jalopy

7. **cotta per qualcuno (avere una)**
   a. to have a crush on someone
   b. to overcook something

8. **della madonna:**
   a. unique
   b. big-time

9. **di fuori (essere)**
   a. to be stood up on a date
   b. to be crazy

10. **faccia tosta**:
    a. nerve, brazenness
    b. red face due to alcohol consumption

11. **fogna (essere una)**:
    a. to smell bad
    b. to be a bottomless pit, said of someone who eats nonstop

12. **lanciarsi:**
    a. to get up one's nerve
    b. to give up

13. **levarsi di torno**:
    a. to be a bottomless pit, to eat nonstop
    b. to leave a place, to "beat it"

14. **lungagnone:**
    a. a tall, thin person, a "beanpole"
    b. a genius

15. **morire dalle risate:**
    a. to die of laughter
    b. to die of hunger

16. **non poterne più**:
    a. to have insomnia
    b. to be unable to take it any longer

17. **paglia**:
    a. cigarette
    b. a very thin person

18. **palla:**
    a. a bore
    b. said of something exciting

19. **sacco**:
    a. a lot, a large quantity
    b. a job that is difficult to perform

20. **scocciare qualcuno:**
    a. to excite someone
    b. to bug someone

21. **secchionaccio:**
    a. bad food
    b. a nerdy bookworm

22. **seminare qualcuno:**
    a. to ditch someone
    b. to bump into someone

23. **sgrifare**:
    a. to wolf down food
    b. to leave quickly

24. **succhiotto:**
    a. hickey
    b. sugar

25. **sull'anima (stare)**:
    a. to annoy
    b. to sleep

26. **tipo:**
    a. difficult job
    b. guy

27. **tirare un bidone**
    a. to stand someone up on a date
    b. to get extremely angry

28. **tirare**:
    a. to smoke
    b. to fall

29. **tirato/a:**
    a. dressed up
    b. stressed out

30. **un accidente**:
    a. a lot
    b. nothing, "zip"

## B. Complete the phrases by choosing the best word from the list below.

BOMBA                    MAIALE
BOTTEGA                  SASSATE
BUCO                     SGOBBARE
FUORI                    SPAZIALE
LANCIARMI                SPENNATO

1. Mi piacerebbe andare al cinema con te, ma devo _____ tutta la notte. Devo presentare una grossa relazione domani mattina.

2. Ogni volta che provo ad aggiustare la mia macchina, faccio un _____ nell'acqua. La prossima volta vado da un meccanico!

3. Mi diverto moltissimo al Luna Park. Che _____!

4. Guarda, l'insegnante ha la _____ aperta! Mi domando se qualcuno in classe avrà il coraggio di dirglielo!

5. Federico ha paura che il ladro lo faccia _____, per il fatto di essere stato testimone oculare del furto.

6. Quella ragazza mi piace molto! Devo _____ perchè voglio invitarla ad uscire con me!

7. Che bel vestito! È davvero _____!

8. Ho mangiato in un ristorante caro, dove mi hanno _____!

9. Raffaele ha mangiato come un _____ alla mia festa. Deve avere un bell'appetito!

10. Non riesco a credere come la gente guidi in questa città. Vanno tutti come le _____!

## C. Match the English phrase in the left column with the Italian translation from the right. Write the appropriate letter in the box.

☐ 1. What's that girl's name? I've been **racking my brain** trying to remember.

☐ 2. I'll never be able to read all these **darned books** in just two days!

☐ 3. I wish I could go with you tonight, but I have **a ton** of work I need to finish.

☐ 4. Luigi dyed his hair orange? **Oh, brother**!

☐ 5. Your father told me the funniest joke. I thought **I was going** to die laughing.

☐ 6. Stop asking me so many questions. You're **really bugging me**!

☐ 7. My new teacher is an old **geezer**. She must be a hundred years old!

☐ 8. I need to buy a new television. Mine is **on the blink**.

☐ 9. Would you like me to give you a **lift** to the market?

☐ 10. Do you know what Franco gave me for my birthday? **Zip**!

A. Vorrei andare con te stasera, ma ho **un casino** di lavoro che devo finire.

B. Tuo padre mi ha raccontato una barzelletta buffissima. Pensavo di **morire dalle risate**.

C. La mia nuova insegnante è una vecchia **babbiona**. Deve avere cent'anni!

D. Sai cosa mi ha regalato Franco per il mio compleanno? **Un accidente**!

E. Vuoi che ti dia uno **strappo** al mercato?

F. Come si chiama quella ragazza? Mi sono **spremuto le meningi**, cercando di ricordare.

G. Smettila di farmi tante domande. Mi **stai** davvero **scocciando**!

H. Non riuscirò mai a leggere queste **scartoffie** in soli due giorni!

I. Devo comparmi una nuova televisione. Quella che ho ora è **kaput**.

J. Luigi si è tinto i capelli d'arancione? **Buona notte**!

## D. Underline the word that best completes the phrase.

1. Quella (**ciospa**, **cispa**, **cialda**) pensa di poter vincere il concorso di bellezza? Deve essere matta!

2. Mi sono divertito moltissimo ieri sera. Che (**pedata**, **fessata**, **figata**)!

3. Angelo prima era muscolosissimo. Ora è un (**buzzino**, **bazzino**, **bustino**).

4. Se non smette di darmi fastidio, lo mando al (**cavolo**, **pendolo**, **diavolo**).

5. (**Azzanna**, **Amara**, **Ammazza**)! Hai visto quel fulmine?

6. Devo comprarmi un nuovo computer. Quello che ho ora è completamente (**casino**, **kaput**, **occhio**).

7. Hai intenzione di andare a piedi fino all'aeroporto? Mi farebbe piacere darti uno (**strappo**, **tappo**, **straccio**)!

8. Sta' attento! Sei quasi passato con il rosso! Vuoi che tu ed io finiamo (**spappolati**, **popolati**, **spennati**)?!

9. Il professore mi ha detto che mi (**sera**, **sega**, **saga**) alla fine dell'anno, se non passo il prossimo esame!

10. Hai sentito (**la prima**, **l'ultima**, **la penultima**)? Massimo si sposa la prossima settimana!

11. L'unico motivo per cui Francesca prende dei buoni voti è perchè lei è la (**protetta**, **barchetta**, **promessa**) dell'insegnante!

12. Non ho visto Alberto a scuola oggi. Mi domando se abbia fatto (**barca**, **porta**, **forca**).

# Il mio vicino è *flippato* e dovrebbe andare da uno *strizzacervelli!*

*(trans.): My neighbor's **nuts** and should go see a **shrink**!*
*(lit.): My neighbor's **flipped** and should go see a **brain squeezer**!*

# LEZIONE SEI · Dialogue in Slang

**Filippo:** Allora, dimmi un po'dei tuoi nuovi vicini. Che tipi sono?

**Giovanna:** Mah, il marito è un vero e proprio **armadio**, ma è anche una gran brava persona. Lui è davvero un gran **figo**, e a dirti la verità, sua moglie è una **racchia** e una **pizza** tremenda. È anche una che non **si cheta** mai – una vera e propria **chiacchierona**! Tempo fa mi diceva che **non avevano un becco d'un quattrino** quando hanno traslocato qui, e ora sono **ricchi sfondati**. Sinceramente, penso che lei sia una gran **ballista**.

**Filippo:** Deve essere **flippato** per aver sposato una **balorda** simile. Penso che dovrebbe andare da uno **strizzacervelli**.

**Giovanna:** E avresti dovuto vedere la loro casa – un vero e proprio **troiaio**! Puzzava **da fare schifo**.

**Filippo:** E chi è quel vecchio **bavoso** con la barba che vedo entrare nella loro casa tutte le volte?

**Giovanna:** Vuoi dire il **barilotto**? Oh, quello è il fratello di Giorgia. Ha soli trentacinque **anni**, ma li **porta malissimo**. Lui è una **frana** e detto fra noi sembra abbastanza **rintronato**.

# My neighbor's nuts and should go see a shrink!

*Filippo:* So, tell me about the new neighbors. What are they like?

*Giovanna:* Well the husband is a **tall and imposing man**, but he's a great guy. He's such a **hunk** and, to be honest, his wife is a real **troll** and a **total bore**. She never stops **blabbing** — she's a real **blabbermouth**! She went on and on about how they **didn't have a red cent** when they first moved here and now they're **rolling in dough**. Frankly, I think she's a **liar**.

*Filippo:* He must be **wacked out** to have married such a **crackpot**. I think he should go see a **shrink**.

*Giovanna:* And you should have seen their house – a real **pigsty**! It really **stunk**.

*Filippo:* Who was the **old fart** with the beard I see walk into their house all the time?

*Giovanna:* You mean the **short, fat guy**? That's Giorgia's brother. He's only thirty-five **years old, but he looks terrible**. He's such a **loser** and frankly, he's **not the sharpest tack on the board**.

# My neighbor's flipped and should go see a *brain squeezer!*

*Filippo:* So, tell me about the new neighbors. What are they like?

*Giovanna:* Well the husband is a **closet**, but he's a great guy. He's such a **hunk** and, to be honest, his wife is a real **ugly person** and a total **pizza**. She never **gets calm** — she's a real **chatterer**! She went on and on about how they **didn't have a beak of a penny** when they first moved here and now they're **rich without bottom**. Frankly, I think she's a **ball-carrier**.

*Filippo:* He must be **wacked out** to have married such a **crackpot**. I think he should go see a **brain-squeezer**.

*Giovanna:* And you should have seen their house – a real and proper **pigsty**! It really **was from making disgust**.

*Filippo:* Who was the **old drooler** with the beard I see walk into their house all the time?

*Giovanna:* You mean the **small keg**? That's Giorgia's brother. He's only thirty-five **badly carried years** old. He's such a **landslide** and frankly, he's **sound-blasted**.

# VOCABULARY

**armadio** *m.* tall and imposing man • (lit.): closet.

> *example:* Filippa è molto piccola e magra, mentre suo marito è un **armadio**.
>
> *translation:* Filippa is very small and thin, but her husband is a **very tall and imposing man**.
>
> **ALSO -1:** **lungagnone** *m.* (as introduced in Lesson Two, p. 29) tall and lanky man • (lit.): from *lungo,* meaning "long."
>
> **ALSO -2:** **pennello** *m.* (Northern & Central Italy) tall man • (lit.): paintbrush.
>
> **VARIATION:** **pennellone** *m.*
>
> **ALSO -3:** **pertica** *f.* • (lit.): pole.
>
> **ALSO -4:** **perticone** *m.* from *pertica,* meaning "pole."
>
> **ALSO -5:** **stanga** *f.* • (lit.): bar.

**ballista** *f.* liar • (lit.): from *balle,* meaning "lies," or literally, "bales."

> *example:* Non puoi credere a niente di quello che Roberto ti dice. Lui è un **ballista**!
>
> *translation:* You can't believe anything Roberto says to you. He's a **liar**!
>
> **NOTE:** **una balla** *f.* a cock-and-bull story.

**balordo/a** *n.* crackpot, nut, blockhead.

> *example:* Sono proprio **balordo**! Oggi ho chiuso la macchina con le chiavi dentro, due volte!
>
> *translation:* I'm such a **blockhead**. I locked my keys in the car for the second time this week!
>
> **SYNONYM:** **baccalà** *m.* • (lit.): dried fish.

**barilotto** *m.* (applied usually only to a man) short, fat man • (lit.): small keg.

> *example:* Aldo è un **barilotto**, mentre sua moglie è alta e snella.
>
> *translation:* Aldo is a **short, fat guy**, but his wife is tall and slender.

**SYNONYM:**   **buzzino** *m.* (as seen in Lesson Five) short, fat man with a potbelly • (lit.): from *buzza,* meaning "belly."

**bavoso/a** *n.* old geezer, old fart • (lit.): drooler (from the verb *sbavare,* meaning "to drool").

    *example:*   Quel vecchio **bavoso** in fondo alla strada era un atleta olimpionico. Da non crederci!

    *translation:*   That **old geezer** down the street used to be an Olympic athlete. It's hard to believe!

    **SYNONYM:**   **babbione/a** *n.*

**becco d'un quattrino (non avere un)** *exp.* not to have a red cent • (lit.): not to have a beak of a penny.

    *example:*   Quando i miei nonni sono arrivati in questo paese, non avevano il **becco d'un quattrino**. Ora invece sono proprietari di un bel negozio.

    *translation:*   When my grandparents came to this country, they **didn't have a red cent**. Now they own a successful business.

    **VARIATION:**   **restare senza il becco d'un quattrino** *exp.* to remain without a beak of a penny.

    **SYNONYM:**   **spennato/a** *adj.* (as introduced in Lesson Three, p. 47) broke • (lit.): plucked.

    **NOTE:**   A *quattrino* was an old coin made of copper in the mid-thirteenth century that had little value, like a penny.

**chetarsi** *v.* to shut up • (lit.): to grow calm, to abate.

    *example:*   In aereo, ero seduto accanto a una signora che non **si è chetata** per tutto il volo!

    *translation:*   On the airplane, I sat next to a woman who wouldn't **shut up** the entire flight!

**chiacchierone/a** *n.* blabbermouth • (lit.): from the verb *chiacchierare,* meaning "to chatter."

    *example:*   C'è Carolina! Se mi vede quella non finisce più di parlare. Lei è così **chiacchierona**!

    *translation:*   There's Carolina! If she sees me, she'll talk forever. She's such a **blabbermouth**!

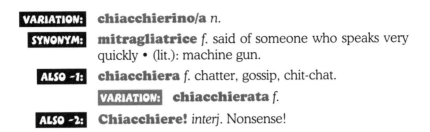

**VARIATION:** **chiacchierino/a** *n.*

**SYNONYM:** **mitragliatrice** *f.* said of someone who speaks very quickly • (lit.): machine gun.

**ALSO -1:** **chiacchiera** *f.* chatter, gossip, chit-chat.

**VARIATION:** **chiacchierata** *f.*

**ALSO -2:** **Chiacchiere!** *interj.* Nonsense!

**da fare schifo** *exp.* said of something disgusting • (lit.): from making disgust.

    *example:* Questo liquore è forte **da fare schifo**!

    *translation:* This liquor is **disgustingly** strong!

**NOTE:** The expression **da fare schifo** always follows an adjective, as opposed to **fare schifo**, also meaning "to be disgusting," which stands alone. For example:

    *example:* Ora capisco perchè questo albergo è così economico. **Fa schifo**!

    *translation:* Now I understand why this hotel is so inexpensive. **It's disgusting**!

**ALSO:** **prendere in schifo** *exp.* to take an immediate dislike to someone or something.

**figo** *m.* handsome guy, hunk.

    *example:* Hai visto il nuovo ragazzo di Giovanna? È così **figo**!

    *translation:* Did you see Giovanna's new boyfriend? He's such a **hunk**!

**VARIATION:** **figone** *m.*

**flippato/a** *adj.* (from English) crazy, flipped out • (lit.): flipped (from the verb *flipparsi*, meaning "to flip out").

    *example:* Come mai quell'uomo sta parlando ad un lampione? Deve essere **flippato**!

    *translation:* Why is that man talking to that lamppost? He must be **flipped out**!

**NOTE:** The adjective *flippato/a* can also be used in slang to mean "flipped out on drugs."

**SYNONYM:** **di fuori (essere)** *exp.* (as introduced in Lesson Two, p. 28) to be crazy • (lit.): to be out (of one's mind).

**frana** *f.* a failure (when referring to a person) • (lit.): landslide.

> *example:* Questa è la terza volta che Franco viene licenziato questo mese. È davvero una **frana**.
>
> *translation:* This is the third time this month that Franco got fired from a job. He's such a **loser**.

**pizza** *f.* a bore • (lit.): pizza.

> *example:* Non andare a vedere quel film! L'ho visto ieri ed era una tale **pizza**!
>
> *translation:* Don't go see that movie! I saw it yesterday and it was a real **bore**!
>
> **SYNONYM -1:** **depressione** *f.* said of anything boring and dull • (lit.): depression.
>
> **SYNONYM -2:** **palla** *f.* (as introduced in Lesson Two, p. 30) a bore, a drag • (lit.): bullet, shot.
>
> **SYNONYM -3:** **piaga** *f.* (Northern & Central Italy) • (lit.): plague.

**portare male gli anni** *exp.* not to be aging well• (lit.): to carry the years badly.

> *example:* Martina ha solo venticinque anni? Ne dimostra sessanta! Li **porta davvero male**.
>
> *translation:* Martina is only twenty-five years old? She looks about sixty! She's **really not aging well**.

**racchia** *f.* said of an extremely ugly girl, a "troll."

> *example:* Federica è una gran **racchia**, mentre i suoi genitori sono veramente belli!
>
> *translation:* Federica is a real **troll**, but her parents are so attractive!
>
> **NOTE:** This can also be used as an adjective, as in *racchio/a*.

**ricco sfondato / ricca sfondata (essere)** *exp.* to be filthy rich • (lit.): to be rich without bottom.

> *example:* Hai visto che macchina cara hanno i genitori di Simona? Devono essere **ricchi sfondati**!
>
> *translation:* Did you see the expensive car Simona's parents have? They must be **mega rich**!

**rintronato/a** *adj.* said of someone who is rather dull, not too bright, not the sharpest tack on the board • (lit.): from the verb *rintronare,* meaning "to make a loud, thunderous noise" (said of someone who looks as if he/she has been stunned from a loud noise or explosion).

> *example:* Ho provato ad insegnare a Sergio ad usare il computer, ma lui non capisce niente! Deve essere un po' **rintronato**.

> *translation:* I tried to explain to Sergio how to use the computer, but he just doesn't get it! He's **not the sharpest tack on the board**.

**strizzacervelli** *m.* (humorous) psychoanalyst, "shrink" • (lit.): from *strizzare,* meaning "to squeeze," and *cervelli,* meaning "brains."

> *example:* – Mia zia pensa di essere una gallina.
> – Perchè non la mandi da uno **strizzacervelli**?
> – Perchè abbiamo bisogno delle uova!

> *translation:* – My aunt thinks she's a chicken!
> – Why don't you send her to a **shrink**?
> – Because we need the eggs!

**troiaio** *m.* pigsty • (lit.): from *troia,* meaning "sow."

> *example:* Hai visto l'appartamento di Marco? È un **troiaio**!

> *translation:* Did you see Marco's apartment? It's a **pigsty**!

# PRACTICE THE VOCABULARY

(Answers to Lesson Six, p. 184)

## A. CROSSWORD
**Fill in the crossword puzzle on page 103 by choosing the correct words from the list.**

| | | |
|---|---|---|
| ANNI | CHIACCHIERONE | RINTRONATO |
| ARMADIO | FIGO | SCHIFO |
| BALLISTA | FLIPPATO | SFONDATO |
| BALORDO | FRANA | STRIZZACERVELLI |
| BARILOTTO | PIZZA | TROIAIO |
| BAVOSO | QUATTRINO | |
| CHETARSI | RACCHIA | |

## ACROSS

20. ____ *m.* (humorous) psychoanalyst, "shrink" • (lit.): from *strizzare,* meaning "to squeeze," and *cervelli,* meaning "brains."

24. **portare male gli** ____ *exp.* not to be aging well• (lit.): to carry the years badly.

36. ____ *f.* said of an extremely ugly girl, a "troll."

43. **becco d'un** ____ **(non avere un)** *exp.* not to have a red cent • (lit.): not to have a beak of a penny.

54. ____ *v.* to shut up • (lit.): to grow calm, to abate.

62. ____ *f.* a failure (when referring to a person) • (lit.): landslide.

64. ____ *n.* old geezer, old fart • (lit.): drooler (from the verb *sbavare,* meaning "to drool").

68. **ricco** ____ **(essere)** *exp.* to be filthy rich • (lit.): to be rich without bottom.

## DOWN

2. ____ *adj.* said of someone who is rather dull, not too bright, not the sharpest tack on the board.

11. ____ *m.* (applied usually only to a man) short, fat man • (lit.): keg.

13. ____ *adj.* (from English) crazy, flipped out • (lit.): flipped (from the verb *flipparsi,* meaning "to flip out").

14. ____ *f.* a bore • (lit.): pizza.

16. ____ *f.* liar • (lit.): from *balle,* meaning "lies," or literally, "bales."

19. ____ *m.* tall and imposing man • (lit.): cupboard, wardrobe.

21. ____ *n.* blabbermouth • (lit.): from the verb *chiacchierare,* meaning "to chatter" or "to talk nonsense."

35. ____ *m.* handsome guy, hunk.

39. ____ *m.* pigsty • (lit.): from *troia,* meaning "sow."

50. **da fare** ____ *exp.* said of something disgusting.

51. ____ *n.* crackpot, nut, blockhead.

# CROSSWORD PUZZLE

## B. Complete the phrases below by choosing the appropriate word from the list.

**ARMADIO**                    **FLIPPATO**
**BAVOSO**                   **RINTRONATO**
**BECCO D'UN QUATTRINO**        **SCHIFO**
**CHIACCHIERONE**          **STRIZZACERVELLI**
**FIGO**                        **TROIAIO**

1. Franco era così piccolo.  Ora è un _____

2. Quel vecchio _____ è tuo vicino di casa?  Deve avere cent'anni!

3. Prima che mi trasferissi qui, questo appartamento era un

   _____.

4. Mio zio è pazzo.  Sono cinque anni che va da uno

   _____.

5. Mio nonno è _____.  Sono anni che va dallo psichiatra.

6. Ti rendi conto quanto parla?  Che _____!

7. Alessio e Gianluca sono fratelli, ma sono così diversi.  Alessio è un brillante scienziato, mentre suo fratello è _____.

8. Antonio deve aver fatto ginnastica per anni.  È diventato un

   _____!

9. Mi piacerebbe venire al cinema con te stasera, ma non ho un

   _____.

10. Questo caffè è amaro da fare_____!

# C. Underline the word that best completes the phrase.

1. Cinzia mi ha detto di essere nobile. Giuro, è così (**ballone**, **ballista**, **balestra**)!

2. Giorgia ha solo trent'anni? Pensavo che ne avesse sessanta! Li (**porta**, **parto**, **parete**) davvero male!

3. Hai visto la (**secchia**, **pacchia**, **racchia**) con cui esce Gabriele? È davvero brutta!

4. Il padre di Marcello è un (**barcotto**, **grullotto**, **barilotto**), mentre Marcello è alto e muscoloso.

5. Povero Saverio. Sono due mesi che non ha un lavoro e non ha un (**becco**, **bacco**, **bricco**) d'un quattrino.

6. Hai visto quel (**fumo**, **pago**, **figo**) che è appena entrato? È bellissimo e ha un corpo stupendo!

7. Quella donna non smette mai di parlare. Che (**carlona**, **chiesona**, **chiacchierona**)!

8. Non mi sono divertito affatto a lezione. Era davvero una (**pizza**, **pazza**, **pozza**)

9. Dovresti vedere che casa ha appena comprato Matteo. È enorme! Deve essere ricco (**sfondato**, **fidanzato**, **sfasato**).

10. La mia vicina di casa parla sempre da sola. Credo che sia (**flippata**, **flipperata**, **fulminata**).

11. È difficile ascoltare il film, perchè la donna dietro di noi parla in continuazione. Le dico di (**chinarsi**, **chetarsi**, **chiacchierare**).

12. Fa schifo qui! Come fai a vivere in questo (**trappola**, **trippaio**, **troiaio**)?

## D. Match the English phrase in the left column with the Italian translation from the right. Write the appropriate letter in the box.

1. Filippa is very small and thin, but her husband is a **very tall and imposing man**.

2. Don't go see that movie! I saw it yesterday and it was a real **bore**!

3. Did you see the expensive car Simona's parents have? They must be **mega rich**!

4. Did you see Giovanna's new boyfriend? He's such a **hunk**!

5. That **old geezer** down the street used to be an Olympic athlete. It's hard to believe!

6. Martina is only twenty-five years old? She looks about sixty! She's **really not aging well**.

7. Matteo is a **short, fat guy**, but his wife is tall and slender.

8. When my grandparents came to this country, they **didn't have a red cent**. Now they own a successful business.

9. This liquor is **disgustingly** strong!

10. George failed the same test three times. What a **loser**!

A. Non andare a vedere quel film! L'ho visto ieri ed era una tale **pizza**!

B. Quel vecchio **bavoso** in fondo alla strada era un atleta olimpionico. Da non crederci!

C. Filippa è molto piccola e magra, mentre suo marito è un **armadio**.

D. Quando i miei nonni sono arrivati in questo Paese non avevano il **becco d'un quattrino**; ora invece sono proprietari di un bel negozio!

E. Giorgio è stato segato per la terza volta allo stesso esame. Che **frana**!

F. Hai visto che macchina cara hanno i genitori di Simona? Devono essere **ricchi sfondati**!

G. Martina ha solo venticinque anni? Ne dimostra sessanta! Li **porta davvero male**.

H. Matteo è un **barilotto**, mentre sua moglie è alta e snella.

I. Hai visto il nuovo ragazzo di Giovanna? È così **figo**!

J. Questo liquore è forte **da fare schifo**!

# E. DICTATION
## Test Your Listening Comprehension

*(This dictation can be found in the Appendix on page 195.)*

If you are following along with your cassette, you will now hear a series of sentences from the opening dialogue. These sentences will be read by a native speaker at normal conversational speed (which may seem fast to you at first). In addition, the words will be pronounced as you would actually hear them in a conversation, often including some common reductions.

The first time the sentences are presented, simply listen in order to get accustomed to the speed and heavy use of reductions. The sentences will then be read again with a pause after each to give you time to write down what you heard. The third time the sentences are read, follow along with what you have written.

# Graziella è davvero diventata una *scorfana*!

(trans.): Graziella has really turned into a **troll**!
(lit.): Graziella has really turned into a **scorpion fish**!

*Martina:* **Ammappa**! Hai visto i prezzi su quei vestiti? Soltanto un **allocco sputtanerebbe** tutti quei **sacchi** per comprarsi dei simili **stracci**. Devi essere davvero **fuori di testa**. Che **fregatura**! C'è qualcosa in questo negozio che ti **tira**?

*Carlotta:* **Per carità**! Nulla! Leviamoci di qui. Sto cercando un vestito da poco.

*Martina:* Ci sono dei bei vestiti in quella vetrina là.

*Carlotta:* L'ultima volta che sono entrata in quel negozio, ci ho **intoppato** Graziella Lariani. Mi sembra che si stia davvero **lasciando andare allo sbraco**! Sembra che stia **pappando** e bevendo un po' troppo. È diventata una vera **balenottera**!

*Martina:* È davvero cambiata così tanto?

*Carlotta:* Sì, è davvero diventata una **scorfana**!

# Graziella has really turned into a *troll!*

*Martina:* **Wow**! Did you see the price of these clothes? Only a **sucker would blow** that kind of **money** for **rags** like this. You'd have to be **out of your mind**. What a **rip-off**! Does anything in this store **strike your fancy**?

*Carlotta:* **Give me a break**! Not a thing. Let's get out of here. I'm looking for an inexpensive dress.

*Martina:* There are some great dresses in that shop over there.

*Carlotta:* The last time I was in that shop, I **bumped into** Graziella Lariani. She's really **letting herself go**! She looks like she **wolfs down food** and drinks a little too much. She's such a **fatso**!

*Martina:* Has she really changed that much?

*Carlotta:* Yes, she's really turned into a **troll**!

# Graziella has really turned into a *scorpion fish!*

Martina: **Wow**! Did you see the price on these clothes? Only an **owl would whore away** those kinds of **sacks** for **rags** like this. You'd have to be **out of head**. What a **swindle**! Does anything in this store **pull you**?

Carlotta: **For charity**! Not a thing! Let's get out of here. I'm looking for an inexpensive dress.

Martina: There are some great dresses in that shop over there.

Carlotta: The last time I was in that shop, I **bumped** Graziella Lariani. She's really **letting herself go sloppy**! She looks like she **wolfs down food** and drinks a little too much. She's such a **fatso**!

Martina: Has she really changed that much?

Carlotta: Yes, she's really turned into a **scorpion fish**!

# VOCABULARY

**allocco/a** *n.* numbskull, idiot • (lit.): owl.

> *example:* Soltanto un **allocco** crederebbe a tutto quelo che dice Mario. Tutti sanno che lui è un bugiardo!

> *translation:* Only an **idiot** would believe anything that Mario says. Everyone knows he's a liar!

**VARIATION:** **alloccone/a** *n.*

**SYNONYM -1:** **babbeo/a** *n.*

**SYNONYM -2:** **fesso/a** *n.* • (lit.): opening.

**SYNONYM -3:** **oca** *f.* (only used in reference to a woman) • (lit.): goose.

**SYNONYM -4:** **scimunito/a** *n.*

**SYNONYM -5:** **sciocco/a** *adj.* • (lit.): bland.

**Ammappa!** *interj.* Wow!

> *example:* **Ammappa**! È la casa più grande che io abbia mai visto!

> *translation:* **Wow**! That's the biggest house I've ever seen!

**SYNONYM -1:** **Ammazza!** *interj.* (as introduced in Lesson Three, p. 51) • (lit.): from the verb *ammazzare,* meaning "to kill" – therefore the closest literal translation could be "Killer!"

**SYNONYM -2:** **Capperi** *interj.* • (lit.): capers.

**SYNONYM -3:** **Cavolo!** *interj.* (as introduced in Lesson One, p. 12) • (lit.): cabbage.

**SYNONYM -4:** **Uah!** *interj.* a variation of the English "Wow!"

**SYNONYM -5:** **Wow!** *interj.* (from English)

**balenottera** *f.* fatso • (lit.): a variation of *balena* (as introduced in Lesson Five, p. 78), meaning "whale."

> *example:* Ora capisco perchè Carlotta è così **balenottera**. Non fa che mangiare!

> *translation:* Now I understand why Carlotta is such a **fatso**. She never stops eating!

**fregatura** *f.* thievery, rip-off.

> *example:* Hai visto il prezzo su quella giacca? Che **fregatura**!
>
> *translation:* Did you see the price for that jacket? What a **rip-off**!

**fuori di testa (essere)** *exp.* to be crazy • (lit.): to be out of one's head.

> *example:* Esci con Martina? Ma sei **fuori di testa**? Lei ha già un ragazzo, per giunta il più grosso della scuola!
>
> *translation:* You're going out with Martina? Are you **out of your mind**? She already has a boyfriend who is the biggest guy in school!

> **SYNONYM -1:** **di fuori (essere)** *exp.* (as introduced in Lesson Two, p. 28) • (lit.): to be out (of one's mind).

> **SYNONYM -2:** **flippato/a** *adj.* (as introduced in Lesson Six, p. 99) • (lit.): flipped.

> **SYNONYM -3:** **girare** *v.* (Central Italy) • (lit.): to turn • *Ma ti gira il cervello?*; Are you nuts? (lit.): Is your brain turning?

**intoppare qualcuno** *v.* to see someone unexpectedly, to bump into someone • (lit.): to bump someone.

> *example:* Non indovinerai mai chi ho **intoppato** oggi – il mio primo ragazzo! Non lo vedevo da vent'anni!
>
> *translation:* You'll never guess whom I **bumped into** today – my first boyfriend! I haven't seen him in twenty years!

**lasciarsi andare allo sbraco** *exp.* to let oneself go • (lit.): to let oneself go sloppy.

> *example:* Franesca si è **lasciata andare allo sbraco**! Era così carina una volta!
>
> *translation:* Francesca has **let herself go**! She used to be so pretty!

**pappare** *v.* to eat, to wolf down food • (lit.): from *pappa*, meaning "baby food."

> *example:* Avevo lasciato un sacco di cibo in frigo, ma Massimo si è **pappato** tutto!
>
> *translation:* I had left a lot of food in the refrigerator, but Massimo **ate** it all!

**per carità** *exp.* "please" when used to mean: **1.** give me a break, "pah-leeze!"; **2.** "Please, I'm begging you!"; **3.** "Please, that's really not necessary" • (lit.): for charity.

> *example -1:* – C'è qualcosa in questo negozio che ti piace?
> – **Per carità**! Nulla!
>
> *translation:* – Is there anything in this store that you like?
> – **Give me a break**! Not a thing!
>
> *example -2:* **Per carità**. Non dire niente a nessuno!
>
> *translation:* **Please, I'm begging you**. Don't tell anyone!
>
> *example -3:* – Posso aiutarti a caricare il tuo furgone con la legna?
> – No, **per carità**. Non devi!
>
> *translation:* – Can I help you load your truck with all this wood?
> – No, **please**. You don't have to!

**sacchi** *m.pl.* a multiple of 1,000 lire, equivalent to about 50 cents • (lit.): sacks (or thousands of lire – For example: *20 sacchi* = 20,000 lire).

> *example:* – Quanto hai pagato questa bicicletta?
> – L'ho pagata 200 **sacchi**!
>
> *translation:* – How much did you pay for this bike?
> – I paid two hundred **thousand lire**!

**scorfana** *f.* an extremely ugly woman, a "troll" • (lit.): from *scorfano*, meaning "scorpion fish."

> *example:* Cinzia era così carina e ora è una **scorfana**! Chissà che le è successo!
>
> *translation:* Cinzia used to be so pretty amd now she's a real **troll**! I wonder what happened to her!
>
> **NOTE:** This term is generally only applied to women.
>
> **SYNONYM:** **racchia** *f.* (as introduced in Lesson Six, p. 100)

**sputtanare** *v.* to blow money, to throw money away • (lit.): from *puttana*, meaning "whore."

> *example:* Enrico compra tutto quelo che vede. **Sputtana** così tanti soldi in un sol giorno!
>
> *translation:* Enrico buys everything he sees. He **blows so much money** in just one day!

**stracci** *m.pl.* old clothes, "threads" • (lit.): rags.

> *example:* Hai visto che **stracci** aveva addosso Chiara a scuola? Stava malissimo!

> *translation:* Did you see the **clothes** Chiara was wearing in school? She looked terrible!

**tirare qualcuno** *v.* to attract or "grab" someone • (lit.): to pull.

> *example:* **Ti tira** questo vestito? Mi piace un sacco!

> *translation:* How does this dress **grab you**? Personally, I love it!

# PRACTICE THE VOCABULARY

*(Answers to Lesson Seven, p. 185)*

## A. Choose the correct definition of the words in boldface. Circle your answer.

1. **fregatura**:
   a. fracture
   b. thievery, rip-off

2. **allocco**:
   a. a genius
   b. a numbskull, idiot

3. **sacchi**:
   a. a multiple of 1,000 lire
   b. a difficult job

4. **tirare qualcuno**:
   a. to attract someone
   b. to repel someone

5. **scorfana**:
   a. a beautiful woman
   b. an extremely ugly woman

6. **fuori di testa (essere)**:
   a. to be excited, thrilled
   b. to be crazy

7. **intoppare qualcuno**:
   a. to kill someone
   b. to see someone unexpectedly

8. **per carità**:
   a. don't bother
   b. I need your help

9. **lasciarsi andare allo sbraco**:
   a. to let oneself go
   b. to let one's hair down and have a great time

10. **sputtanare**:
    a. to blow money
    b. to spit

11. **stracci**:
    a. shoes
    b. old clothes

12. **pappare**:
    a. to eat
    b. to talk

## B. Complete the following phrases by filling in the blanks with the appropriate words from the list below.

| | |
|---|---|
| BALENOTTERA | SBRACO |
| FREGATURA | SCOPPIATA |
| INTOPPATO | SCORFANA |
| PAPPARE | SPUTTANATO |
| SACCHI | TIRA |

1. Niente mi _____ in questo negozio. Andiamo da qualche altra parte.

2. Hai _____ tutti i tuoi soldi in un nuovo vestito?

3. Hai pagato duecento _____ per una penna?! Sei pazzo?

4. È così caro. Che _____!

5. Dove vorresti andare a _____ stasera?

6. Roberta era davvero carina una volta, ma ultimamente si è lasciata andare allo _____.

7. Quella donna là sta urlando a se stessa. Credo che sia un pò _____.

8. Oggi ho _____ il mio vecchio ragazzo. È diventato davvero grasso!

9. Se continui a mangiare dolci tutto il tempo, diventerai una _____.

10. Cristina era carina una volta! Che le è successo? Ora è proprio una _____!

## C. FIND-A-WORD PUZZLE
**Using the list below, circle the words in the grid on the opposite page that are missing from the definition below. The words may be spelled vertically or horizontally.**

| | |
|---|---|
| **ALLOCCO** | **SACCHI** |
| **AMMAPPA** | **SBRACO** |
| **BALENOTTERA** | **SCORFANA** |
| **CARITÀ** | **SPUTTANARE** |
| **FREGATURA** | **STRACCI** |
| **INTOPPARE** | **TESTA** |
| **PAPPARE** | **TIRARE** |

1. _____ **qualcuno** *v.* to bump into someone.

2. _____ *f.* fatso.

3. _____ *f.* thievery, rip-off.

4. _____ **qualcuno** *v.* to attract someone.

5. _____ *v.* to blow money.

6. _____ *m.pl.* clothes, "threads."

7. _____! *interj.* Wow!

8. **fuori di** _____ **(essere)** *exp.* to be crazy.

9. **lasciarsi andare allo** _____ *exp.* to let oneself go.

10. _____ *f.* an extremely ugly woman.

11. _____ *v.* to eat.

12. _____ *m.* numbskull, idiot.

13. _____ *m.pl.* a multiple of 1,000 lire.

14. **per** _____ *exp.* "please" when used to mean **1.** give me a break, "pah-leeze!"; **2.** "Please, I'm begging you!"; **3.** "Please, that's really not necessary" • (lit.): for charity.

## FIND-A-WORD PUZZLE

```
Ù I A A H S E R N A Q A T Y A I
A A R C O A T E O A C O R S O R
S T R A C C I A A L A T T C H E
A H R I T I E L S U R O H O O A
C I E D E R F Y B P E B I R W L
C N A E S A E F R O Y A B F B L
F K I N T O P P A R E L A A O Y
R T L T A E A N C B O E L N R D
E H Y E N G P N O U U N E A I O
G A A A D O P P A R A O N I N E
A T T R I T A Y O I G T O N G A
T Ù I A C A R I T À O A T O T L
U M R A N I E L F O G S T N H L
R U A B A Ù H I F N O A E O I O
A S R B N D E T F O I C R I S C
M C E I A A I J I W N C A Ù I C
L L A M M A P P A W G H A D S O
P S P U T T A N A R E I M E A A
Y P E I B R T H E R E C S N O W
```

# D. Match the English phrase in the left column with the Italian translation from the right. Write the appropriate letter in the box.

1. Only an **idiot** would believe anything that Mario says. Everyone knows he's a liar!

2. Francesca has really **let herself go**!

3. Cinzia used to be so pretty and now she's a real **troll**! I wonder what happened to her!

4. You're going out with Mariella? Are you **out of your mind**? She already has a boyfriend who is the biggest guy in school!

5. Did you see the price on that jacket? What a **rip-off**!

6. Did you see the **old clothes** Chiara was wearing in school? She looked terrible!

7. How does this dress **grab you**? Personally, I love it!

8. I **bumped into** my ex-girlfriend today at Mario's wedding.

9. **Wow**! That's the biggest house I've ever seen!

10. Now I understand why Carlotta is such a **fatso**. She never stops eating!

A. **Ammappa**! È la casa più grande che io abbia mai visto!

B. Cinzia era così carina, e ora è una **scorfana**! Chissà che le è successo!

C. **Ti tira** questo vestito? Mi piace un sacco!

D. Soltanto un **allocco** crederebbe a tutto quelo che dice Mario. Tutti sanno che lui è un bugiardo!

E. Hai visto il prezzo su quella giacca? Che **fregatura**!

F. Francesca si è davvero **lasciata andare allo sbraco**!

G. Esci con Mariella? Ma sei **fuori di testa**? Lei ha già un ragazzo, per giunta il più grosso della scuola!

H. Hai visto che **stracci** aveva addosso Chiara a scuola? Stava malissimo!

I. Oggi ho **intoppato** la mia ex-ragazza al matrimonio di Mario.

J. Ora capisco perchè Carlotta è così **balenottera**. Non fa che mangiare!

## E. DICTATION
## Test Your Listening Comprehension

*(This dictation can be found in the Appendix on page 196.)*

If you are following along with your cassette, you will now hear a series of sentences from the opening dialogue. These sentences will be read by a native speaker at normal conversational speed (which may seem fast to you at first). In addition, the words will be pronounced as you would actually hear them in a conversation, often including some common reductions.

The first time the sentences are presented, simply listen in order to get accustomed to the speed and heavy use of reductions. The sentences will then be read again with a pause after each to give you time to write down what you heard. The third time the sentences are read, follow along with what you have written.

# Pensavo che Oreste fosse una *pasta d'uomo*.

*(trans.): I used to think Oreste was a **good egg**.*
*(lit.): I used to think Oreste was a **dough of a man**.*

**Luigi:** Hai sentito che è successo a Oreste Santovini?

**Sergio:** Vuoi dire il nuovo impiegato? No, che gli è successo?

**Luigi:** Fra noi, **a quattr'occhi**, credo che sarà licenziato. Su questo **non ci piove**.

**Sergio:** E perchè?

**Luigi:** Quando l'ho visto la prima volta, ho pensato che fosse una **pasta d'uomo** e veramente **in gamba** nel suo lavoro. I primi due giorni ha lavorato **a tutta birra**, poi ha cominciato a **perdere colpi** e ora sembra soltanto una **cariatide**. **Cincischia** e **non fa un fico** tutto il giorno. Sono io quello che deve **farsi il culo** perchè io finisco per fare anche il suo!

**Sergio:** Ha veramente **preso in giro** il capo. Mi sorprende che sia stato così **fesso**. A dire il vero fin dal primo momento ho pensato che fosse un po'**fasullo**.

**Luigi:** Il **capoccia gli ha dato una ripassata** perchè qualcuno gli ha **fatto una soffiata** che Oreste veniva a **sfacchinare** completamente **ciucco**!

# I've always thought Oreste was a *good egg.*

*Luigi:*     Did you hear what happened to Oreste Santovini?

*Sergio:*     You mean the new employee? No, what happened to him?

*Luigi:*     **Just between you and me**, I think he's going to get fired. **I'll bet my life on it**.

*Sergio:*     Why?

*Luigi:*     When I first met him, I thought he was a **good egg** and really **skilled** in his work. For the first two days he worked **very hard**, then his work **went downhill** and now he's just **deadweight**. He **wastes his time** and **doesn't do squat** all day. I **bust my butt** because I end up doing his job!

*Sergio:*     He really **took the boss for a ride**. I'm surprised he was such an **idiot**. Frankly, I thought he was a **phony** the moment I met him.

*Luigi:*     The **boss called him on the carpet** because someone **tipped him off** that Oreste was coming to **work totally plastered**!

# I've always thought Oreste was a *dough* of a man.

*Luigi:* Did you hear what happened to Oreste Santovini?

*Sergio:* You mean the new employee? No, what?

*Luigi:* **At four eyes**, I think he's going to get fired. **It's not raining on that**.

*Sergio:* Why?

*Luigi:* When I first met him, I thought he was a **dough of a man** and really **in leg** in his work. The first two days he worked **at full beer**, then his work **took strokes** and now he's just **a stone column**. He **dawdles** and **doesn't do a fig** all day. I **do my ass** because I end up doing his job!

*Sergio:* He really **took the boss for a ride**. I'm surprised he was so **split**. Frankly, I thought he was **false** the moment I met him.

*Luigi:* The **chief gave him a revision** because someone **did the blow** that Oreste was coming to **work totally plastered**!

# VOCABULARY

**a quattr'occhi** *exp.* just between you and me • (lit.): at four eyes.

> *example:* Fra noi, **a quattr'occhi**, ho saputo che Sergio vede un'altra donna all'insaputa di sua moglie.
>
> *translation:* **Just between you and me**, I heard that Sergio is seeing another woman and his wife doesn't suspect!
>
> **NOTE:** Although it may seem redundant, *fra noi,* meaning "between us," usually precedes the expression *a quattr' occhi,* as seen in the above example.

**a tutta birra** *adv.* with great energy, at full throttle • (lit.): at full beer (referring to the "energetic" bubbling of the beer's foam).

> *example:* Dobbiamo metterci a lavorare a **tutta birra** se vogliamo finire questo lavoro per le 5:00!
>
> *translation:* We have to work **full throttle** if we want to finish this job by 5:00!
>
> **SYNONYM -1:** **a palla** *adv.* • (lit.): like a ball (of energy).
>
> **SYNONYM -2:** **a tutto gas** *adv.* • (lit.): at full gasoline.

**capoccia** *m.* boss, foreman, head of the house • (lit.): from *capo,* meaning head, chief, leader, etc.

> *example:* Luigi mi ha fatto chiamare dal **capoccia** per essere arrivato tardi a lavoro.
>
> *translation:* Luigi reported me to the **boss** for arriving late to work.

**cariatide** *f.* said of a person who just stands there and doesn't offer to help, deadweight • (lit.): caryatid (a supporting column carved in the shape of a person).

> *example:* Guido ed io abbiamo fatto tutto il lavoro, mentre Aldo stava lì a guardare! Lui non è altro che una **cariatide**!
>
> *translation:* Guido and I did all the work while Aldo just stood there watching! He's nothing but **deadweight**!

**ciucco/a** *adj.* drunk, plastered.

     *example:*    Sergio è venuto a casa mia completamente **ciucco**!

   *translation:*    Sergio came to my house totally **plastered**!

  **SYNONYM -1:**    **avvinazzato/a** *adj.* (from *vino*, meaning "wine").

  **SYNONYM -2:**    **briaco/a** *adj.* (a Tuscan variation of *ubriaco*, meaning "inebriated").

            **VARIATION:**    **briaco fradicio / briaca fradicia** *exp.* stinking drunk, totally plastered • (lit.): rotten drunk.

  **SYNONYM -3:**    **brillo/a** *adj.* • (lit.): shiny.

  **SYNONYM -4:**    **sbronzo/a** *adj.*

        **ALSO:**    **prendere una ciucca** *exp.* to get very drunk • *Se bevo più di un bicchiere di vino, mi prendo una ciucca;* If I drink more than one glass of wine, I get plastered.

**cincischiare** *v.* to waste time doing nothing productive • (lit.): to chop; to dawdle.

     *example:*    Invece di darsi da fare per trovare un lavoro, Simona se ne è andata in giro a **cincischiare**.

   *translation:*    Instead of looking for a job, Simona just **hung out and did nothing**.

  **SYNONYM:**    **gingillarsi** *v.* • (lit.): to fiddle, to loaf.

**dare/fare una ripassata a qualcuno** *exp.* to reprimand someone, to rake someone over the coals, to call someone on the carpet • (lit.): to give/do someone a revision.

     *example:*    Laura **ha dato una ripassata a suo figlio** perchè lui le aveva detto una bugia.

   *translation:*    Laura **raked her son over the coals** for lying to her.

  **SYNONYM -1:**    **dare/fare una cazziata a qualcuno** *exp.*

  **SYNONYM -2:**    **dare/fare una cazziatone a qualcuno** *exp.*

  **SYNONYM -3:**    **dare/fare una lavata di capo a qualcuno** *exp.* to give a raking over the coals to someone • (lit.): to give/do someone a washing of the head.

  **SYNONYM -4:**    **dare/fare una ramanzina a qualcuno** *exp.* • (lit.): to give/do someone a telling off.

**fare una soffiata** *exp.* to report someone, to rat on someone, "to blow the whistle on someone" • (lit.): to do the blow (from the verb *soffiare*, meaning "to blow").

> **SYNONYM -1:** **fare una spifferata** *exp.* • (lit.): to do a gust.
>
> *example:* Come ha fatto a sapere il capo che tu sei arrivato a lavoro tardi oggi? Qualcuno ha **fatto una soffiata**?
>
> *translation:* How did the boss find out you came in late today? Did someone **snitch**?

**farsi il culo** *exp.* to work extremely hard, to bust one's butt • (lit.): to do one's ass.

> *example:* **Mi sono fatto il culo** per tre mesi, per cercare di finire il progetto. Ho perfino lavorato durante i fine settimana, ma il capo non mi ha nemmeno ringraziato!
>
> *translation:* I **busted my butt** for three months in order to get this project done. I even worked on weekends and the boss didn't even thank me!
>
> **NOTE:** Remember, although this expression uses the masculine noun *culo*, literally meaning "ass," its connotation is <u>not</u> as strong as in English. It is important to remember that by European standards, Americans are considered somewhat prudish and many terms that would be considered highly offensive in the United Sates are quite acceptable in other countries such as Italy.
>
> **SYNONYM:** **darci dentro** *exp.* to work or study very hard • (lit.): to give oneself inside.

**fasullo** • **1.** *adj.* phony • **2.** *m.* a fake, a faker.

> *example:* Non mi fido di Massimo, perchè penso che sia un po' **fasullo**!
>
> *translation:* I don't trust Massimo. I think he's a little **phony**.

**fesso/a** *n.* jerk, dimwit, dolt, fool • (lit.): from the verb *fendere*, meaning "to split" – therefore, a rough translation could be "someone who is split in the head" or "someone who has half a brain."

> *example:* Marcello è un esperto di automobili. Non riesco veramente a credere che sia stato così **fesso** a comprare quella carcassa per 5.000 dollari!
>
> *translation:* Marcello is a car expert. I am really surprised that he was so **stupid** to buy a wreck for $5,000!

**NOTE:** In large numbers, the comma is used in English whereas in Italian, the period is used. For example: *(English)* 5,000 = *(Italian)* 5.000.

**in gamba (essere)** *exp.* to be on the ball • (lit.): to be in leg.

> *example:* Alessio è un bravissimo medico. Lui riesce a fornire diagnosi più accurate di quelle della maggior parte degli altri medici. È davvero **in gamba**!
>
> *translation:* Alessio is a great doctor. He can diagnose a patient more accurately than most doctors. He's really **on the ball**!

**non ci piove** *exp.* I'd bet my life on it • (lit.): It's not raining on that.

> *example:* Il capo ha appena chiamato Pasquale nel suo ufficio. Penso che lo licenzierà. **Non ci piove**!
>
> *translation:* The boss just called Pasquale into his office. I think he's going to get fired. **I'd bet my life on it**!

**non fare un fico** *exp.* not to do a darn thing, not to do an iota • (lit.): not to do a fig.

> *example:* Uno di questi giorni Giuseppe verrà licenziato. **Non fa un fico** tutto il giorno!
>
> *translation:* One of these days, Giuseppe is going to get fired. He **doesn't do a darn thing** all day!
>
> **SYNONYM:** **non fare un tubo** *exp.* • (lit.): not to do a pipe.

**pasta d'uomo** *f.* a nice guy, a good egg • (lit.): dough of man.

> *example:* Mi piace davvero Davide. Ieri mi ha aiutato ad imbiancare tutta la casa. È proprio **una pasta d'uomo**!
>
> *translation:* I really like David. He helped me paint my entire house yesterday. He's really a **good egg**!

**perdere colpi** *exp.* said of someone or something whose performance is diminishing, to go downhill • (lit.): to lose strokes.

> *example:* Sapevo che Marcello era malato, ma pensavo che stesse meglio. Sono rimasto così sorpreso quando ho saputo che **perdeva colpi**.
>
> *translation:* I knew Marcello was sick, but I thought he was doing better. I was so surprised to hear that he's **going downhill**.

**prendere qualcuno in giro** *exp.* to pull the wool over someone's eyes (either in a deceitful way or in fun) • (lit.): to take someone for a ride.

> *example:* Mi sono fidata di Elena, ma per tutto questo tempo mi ha mentito. Non riesco a credere che **mi abbia preso in giro**!
>
> *translation:* I really trusted Elena but all this time she was lying to me. I can't believe that she **pulled the wool over my eyes**!
>
> **SYNONYM -1:** **prendere per i fondelli** *exp.* • (lit.): to take by the bottom parts.
>
> **SYNONYM -2:** **prendere per il bavero** *exp.* • (lit.): to take by the collar.

**sfacchinare** *v.* to work hard • (lit.): to work hard like a porter (from the masculine noun *facchino*, meaning "porter").

> *example:* Ho **sfacchinato** per sei mesi e il mio capo mi ha licenziato soltanto perchè sono arrivato tardi ieri!
>
> *translation:* I **worked really hard** for six months and my boss fired me because I came in late yesterday!
>
> **SYNONYM:** **sgobbare** *v.* (as introduced in Lesson One, p. 14) • to work hard (from *gobba*, meaning "hump," representing a heavy load being carried on one's shoulders or back).

# PRACTICE THE VOCABULARY

*(Answers to Lesson Eight, p. 187)*

## A. Choose the correct synonym of the word(s) in boldface.

1. **cariatide**:
   a. deadweight (said of a person)
   b. a person who is very uptight

2. **sfacchinare**:
   a. to work hard
   b. to sleep

3. **pasta d'uomo**:
   a. noodle and egg dish
   b. a nice guy, a good egg

4. **in gamba (essere)**:
   a. to run quickly
   b. to be on the ball

5. **non fare un fico**:
   a. not to do a darn thing
   b. not to stick to one's diet

6. **fasullo**:
   a. a fake, faker
   b. an exceptionally tall woman

7. **fare una soffiata**:
   a. to report someone, to be a snitch
   b. to take a nap

8. **dare una ripassata a qualcuno**:
   a. to reprimand someone
   b. to give someone a black eye

9. **farsi il culo**:
   a. to work extremely hard
   b. to talk nonstop

10. **cincischiare**:
    a. to eat
    b. to waste time doing nothing productive

11. **fesso**:
    a. genius
    b. stupid

12. **ciucco**:
    a. crazy
    b. drunk

13. **prendere qualcuno in giro**:
    a. to fall in love with someone
    b. to pull the wool over someone's eyes

14. **perdere colpi**:
    a. said of someone or something whose performance is diminishing, to go downhill
    b. said of someone who complains constantly

15. [fra noi,] **a quattr'occhi**:
    a. just between you and me
    b. someone who wears glasses, "four-eyes"

## B. Complete the phrases below by choosing the appropriate word from the list.

**BIRRA**
**CAPOCCIA**
**CARIATIDE**
**CULO**
**FICO**

**GAMBA**
**GIRO**
**PIOVE**
**QUATTR'OCCHI**
**RIPASSATA**

1. Dobbiamo metterci a lavorare a tutta _____, se vogliamo finire questo lavoro per le 5:00!

2. Mi sono fidata di Elena, ma per tutto questo tempo mi ha mentito. Non riesco a credere che mi abbia preso in _____!

3. Uno di questi giorni Giuseppe verrà licenziato. Non fa un _____ tutto il giorno!

4. Alessio è un bravissimo medico. Lui riesce a fornire diagnosi più accurate di quelle della maggior parte degli altri medici. È davvero in _____!

5. A _____, ho saputo che Sergio vede un'altra donna all'insaputa di sua moglie.

6. Luigi mi ha fatto chiamare dal _____ per essere arrivato tardi a lavoro.

7. Il capo ha appena chiamato Pasquale nel suo ufficio. Scommetto che lo licenzierà. Non ci _____!

8. Laura ha dato una _____ a suo figlio perchè lui le aveva detto una bugia.

9. Mi sono fatto il _____per tre mesi, per cercare di finire il progetto. Ho perfino lavorato durante i fine settimana, ma il capo non mi ha nemmeno ringraziato!

10. Guido ed io abbiamo fatto tutto il lavoro, mentre Aldo stava lì a guardare! Lui non è altro che una _____!

## C. Underline the word that best completes the phrase.

1. Fra noi, a quattr' (**pidocchi, sciocchi, occhi**), ho appena saputo che Massimo verrà licenziato oggi.

2. Il mio ospite non fa altro che guardare la tivvù tutto il giorno. Lui è davvero una (**carota, cariatide, carie**)!

3. Il mio (**capoccia, pancia, boccia**) mi ha appena dato un aumento!

4. Lavoro a tutta (**birra, bara, sbirro**) da due settimane per finire in tempo.

5. Ho creduto a Marco, ma lui mi ha preso in (**giostra, giro, ghiro**).

6. Mi piace un sacco Giorgio. È proprio una (**pizza, palla, pasta**) d'uomo.

7. Carlotta è di nuovo in ospedale? Pensavo che stesse meglio. Sono rimasto così sorpreso quando ho saputo che perdeva (**colpi, calci, corpi**).

8. Samuele è così (**fesso, finto, lesso**). Ha messo del sale nel suo caffè, pensando che fosse zucchero!

9. Penso che Ornella oggi mollerà Enrico. Non ci (**piange, piovra, piove**).

10. Il marito di Sonia non fa un (**becco, fico, micio**) tutto il giorno. È così pigro!

11. Donatella ha dato una (**scheggiata, ribollita, ripassata**) al suo ragazzo perchè si era dimenticato del suo compleanno.

12. Mi sono fatto il (**culo, mulo, rullo**) per preparare la cena per Otello, e lui non mi ha nemmeno ringraziato.

## D. Complete the dialogue using the list below.

| | | |
|---|---|---|
| **BIRRA** | **CULO** | **OCCHI** |
| **CAPOCCIA** | **FASULLO** | **PASTA** |
| **CARIATIDE** | **FESSO** | **PIOVE** |
| **CINCISCHIA** | **FICO** | **RIPASSATA** |
| **CIUCCO** | **GAMBA** | **SFACCHINARE** |
| **COLPI** | **GIRO** | **SOFFIATA** |

*Luigi:*   Hai sentito che è successo a Oreste Santovini?

*Sergio:*   Vuoi dire il nuovo impiegato? No, che gli è successo?

*Luigi:*   Fra noi, **a quattr'**_____, credo che sarà licenziato. Su questo **non ci** _____.

*Sergio:*   E perchè?

*Luigi:*   Quando l'ho visto la prima volta, ho pensato che fosse una _____ **d'uomo** e veramente **in** _____ nel suo lavoro. I primi due giorni ha lavorato **a tutta** _____, poi ha cominciato a **perdere** _____ e ora sembra soltanto una _____. _____ e **non fa un** _____ tutto il giorno. Sono io quello che deve **farsi il** _____ perchè io finisco per fare anche il suo!

*Sergio:*   Ha veramente **preso in** _____ il capo. Mi sorprende che sia stato così _____. A dire il vero fin dal primo momento ho pensato che fosse un po'_____.

*Luigi:*   Il _____ gli ha **dato una** _____ perchè qualcuno gli ha **fatto una** _____ che Oreste veniva a _____ completamente _____!

# E. DICTATION
## Test Your Listening Comprehension

*(This dictation can be found in the Appendix on page 196.)*

If you are following along with your cassette, you will now hear a series of sentences from the opening dialogue. These sentences will be read by a native speaker at normal conversational speed (which may seem fast to you at first). In addition, the words will be pronounced as you would actually hear them in a conversation, often including some common reductions.

The first time the sentences are presented, simply listen in order to get accustomed to the speed and heavy use of reductions. The sentences will then be read again with a pause after each to give you time to write down what you heard. The third time the sentences are read, follow along with what you have written.

# Paolo si è sentito a pezzi ieri.

*(trans.): Paolo was **exhausted** yesterday.*
*(lit.): Paolo was **in pieces** yesterday.*

*Federico:*  Come va? **È una vita** che non ci vediamo! Stai bene?

*Paolo:*  **Mah**. **Non ho carburato** per una settimana. All'inizio **mi sentivo soltanto un po'giù**, poi le cose sono peggiorate. Ho capito di essermi **buscato** l'influenza e allora sono **andato in tilt**. Ho avuto un maledetto mal di testa, mi sono sentito **a pezzi**, e per poco non ho **fatto i gattini**. Ho avuto quasi l'impressione di essere **arrivato al capolinea**.

*Federico:*  Mi dispiace, ma sono felice di vederti **in palla di nuovo**.

*Paolo:*  Figurati! **Mi ero così scocciato** a starmene **ibernato** in casa tutta la settimana.

*Federico:*  Ho un'idea. Andiamoci a vedere un film al cinema qui dietro l'angolo. Ci divertiremo un casino! Quel film deve essere **la fine del mondo**.

*Paolo:*  **Okappa**! Spero soltanto che non sia uno di quei film dove tutti finiscono **impiombati**. Ma le commedie mi piacciono **da matti**!

*Federico:*  Anche a me. Poi, dopo il film possiamo andare al ritrovo qui vicino, a **farci una bevutina**. Ti consiglio comunque di non prenderci niente da **sgranocchiare**, perchè il cibo lì è davvero una **sboba**.

# Paolo was *exhausted* yesterday.

*Federico:*  How are you doing? **It's been a long time** since we've seen each other! Are you okay?

*Paolo:*  **So-so**. **I didn't feel well** for a week. At first I just felt sort of **blah**, then it got worse. Then I realized that I **caught** the flu and was **totally out of it**. I had a terrible headache, I was **exhausted**, and I almost **barfed**. I thought I was at **death's door**.

*Federico:*  I'm sorry to hear it, but I'm glad to see that you're **back on your feet again**.

*Paolo:*  You said it! **I was so bored** having to be **cooped up in my house** all week.

*Federico:*  I have an idea. Let's go see a movie at the theater around the corner. We'll have a blast! The movie is supposed to be **awesome**.

*Paolo:*  **Okay**. I just hope it's not a movie where everyone gets **shot up**. But I love comedies **big-time**!

*Federico:*  Me, too. Then after the movie, we can go to the hangout next door and get a **drink**. Just don't get anything to **eat** there because the food is **slop**.

# Paolo was *in pieces* yesterday.

*Federico:* How are you doing? **It's a life** since we've seen each other! Are you okay?

*Paolo:* **Feh**. **I didn't carburate** for a week. At first I just felt sort of **down** then it got worse. Then I realized that I **found myself** the flu and **went on tilt**. I had a terrible headache, my stomach was **in pieces**, and I almost **made the kittens**. I thought I was **at the terminal**.

*Federico:* I'm sorry to hear it, but I'm glad to see that you're **in ball again**.

*Paolo:* Just imagine! **I was bothering myself so much** having to **hibernate in my house** all week.

*Federico:* I have an idea. Let's go see a movie at the theater around the corner. We'll have a blast! The movie is supposed to be **the end of the world**.

*Paolo:* **Okay**. I just hope it's not a movie where everyone gets **filled up with lead**. But I love comedies **to madness**!

*Federico:* Me, too. Then after the movie, we can go to the hangout next door and **make ourselves a little drink**. Just don't get anything to **nibble** there because the food is **slop**.

# VOCABULARY

**andare in tilt** *exp.* not to be oneself, to be out of it • (lit.): to feel on tilt (said of an arcade game that is nonfunctional).

> *example:* **Mi sento in tilt**. Spero di non prendermi l'influenza!
>
> *translation:* **I feel out of it**. I hope I'm not catching the flu!
>
> **VARIATION:** **fare tilt/sentirsi in tilt** *exp.* • (lit.): to do tilt/to feel in tilt.

**arrivare al capolinea** *exp.* to be at death's door • (lit.): to arrive at the terminal.

> *example:* – Non ti vedo da una settimana! Dove sei stato?
> – Ero a casa con l'influenza! Pensavo di essere **arrivato al capolinea**!
>
> *translation:* – I haven't seen you for a week! Where have you been?
> – I was sick at home with the flu. I thought I was **at death's door**!
>
> **SYNONYM:** **essere alla frutta** *exp.* • (lit.): to be at the fruit.

**buscarsi** *v.* to catch something unpleasant • (lit.): to find oneself.

> *example:* Mi farebbe piacere venire con te al cinema, ma ieri **mi sono buscato** un raffreddore e farei meglio a starmene a casa.
>
> *translation:* I'd like to go with you to the movies but yesterday I **caught** a cold and should probably just stay home.

**carburare** *v.* to feel well • (lit.): to carburate.

> *example:* **Non carburo**. Penso che dovrei andare a casa e mettermi a letto.
>
> *translation:* **I don't feel well**. I think I'd better go home and go to bed.

**fare i gattini** *exp.* to vomit, to barf • (lit.): to make the kittens.

> *example:* Ho dei disturbi di stomaco. Spero di non **fare i gattini** proprio qui al cinema!
>
> *translation:* My stomach is upset. I hope I don't **barf** right here in the movie theater!

**farsi una bevutina** *exp.* to have a drink • (lit.): to make oneself a little drink (from *bevuta*, meaning "a drink").

> *example:* Vogliamo andare a **farci una bevutina** prima di andare al cine?
>
> *translation:* Would you like to go **get a drink** before we go to the movie?

**fine del mondo (la)** *exp.* fantastic, awesome, out of this world • (lit.): the end of the world.

> *example:* Paolo mi ha portato a un ottimo ristorante per il mio compleanno. Il cibo era **la fine del mondo**!
>
> *translation:* Paolo took me to a great restaurant for my birthday. The food was **out of this world**!

**ibernarsi** *v.* to stay cooped up in one place • (lit.): to hibernate.

> *example:* Perchè non vieni a ballare con noi stasera? Non sei stanco di startene **ibernato** in casa tutto il giorno?
>
> *translation:* Why don't you join us tonight and go dancing? Aren't you tired of being **cooped up** in your house all day?

**impiombare** *v.* to shoot someone dead • (lit.): to fill with lead (from the verb *piombare*, meaning "to cover with lead").

> *example:* Sono così stufo dei western dove alla fine tutti finiscono **impiombati**.
>
> *translation:* I'm so tired of westerns where everyone ends up getting **shot dead**.

**macello (un)** *exp.* a lot, big-time • (lit.): a slaughter.

> *example:* Ci divertiremo **un macello** stasera alla festa di carnevale di Lucia!
>
> *translation:* We're going to have fun **big-time** tonight at Lucia's carnival party!

**mah** *adv.* so-so.

    *example:* – Come ti senti oggi?
            – **Mah**. Stavo meglio la settimana scorsa.

    *translation:* – How are you doing today?
              – **So-so**. Last week I actually felt better.

    **NOTE:** "**Mah**" is also used to mean "I don't know."


**matti (da)** *adv.* big-time • (lit.): from madness (as in "to go mad over something").

    *example:* – Ti piace la cioccolata?
            – **Da matti**!

    *translation:* – Do you like chocolate?
              – **Big-time**!

    **SYNONYM -1:** **alla grande** *exp.* (as introduced in Lesson Five, p. 77) • (lit.): to the big.

    **SYNONYM -2:** **da morire** *adj.* (used to modify a noun or verb – as introduced in Lesson Four, p. 60) big-time • (lit.): to die from.

    **SYNONYM -3:** **della madonna** *exp.* (as introduced in Lesson Two, p. 28) big-time, in a major way • (lit.): of the Madonna.

    **SYNONYM -4:** **il massimo** *exp.* • (lit.): the maximum • *Questa pizza è il massimo!;* This pizza is the best!


**nuovo (di)** *adv.* again • (lit.): of new.

    *example:* Quando ho chiamato Gigi, la linea era occupata. Riproverò **di nuovo** più tardi.

    *translation:* When I telephoned Gigi, the line was busy. I'll try **again** later.


**okappa** *interj.* (from English) okay.

    *example:* – Vuoi venire al cinema con me stasera?
            – **Okappa**, ma non posso fare tardi perchè devo cominciare a lavorare presto domattina.

    *translation:* – Do you want to come with me to the movies tonight?
            – **Okay**, but I can't stay out too late because I have to work early in the morning.

**palla (essere in)** *exp.* to be in tip-top shape, to be back on one's feet • (lit.): to be in ball.

> *example:*  Sono stato male per una settimana, ma ora sono nuovamente **in palla**!
>
> *translation:*  I was sick for a week, but I'm finally **back on my feet**.

**pezzi (essere a)** *exp.* to be exhausted (or "to be a nervous wreck" depending on the context) • (lit.): to be in pieces.

> *example:*  Devo schiacciare un sonnellino. Sono **a pezzi**!
>
> *translation:*  I need to take a nap. I'm **wiped out**!

**sboba** *f.* bad food, "slop."

> *example:*  Hai assaggiato la **sboba** che Federica ha preparato ieri sera? Era tremenda!
>
> *translation:*  Did you taste the **slop** Federica made last night? It was horrible!
>
> **VARIATION:**  **sbobba** *f.*

**scocciarsi** *v.* to be bored • (lit.): to bother oneself.

> *example:*  **Mi** ero così **scocciato** durante la lezione!
>
> *translation:*  I was really **bored** during the lecture!
>
> **NOTE:**  You may remember that *scocciare* was presented in Lesson Two on page 30. As demonstrated early in its non-reflexive form, *scocciare qualcuno* means "to bug someone." However, in its reflexive form, *scocciarsi* takes on the meaning "to be bored."
>
> **ALSO -1:**  **scocciatore** *m.* / **scocciatrice** *f.* an annoying person • *Che scocciatore quello!*; What a pain in the neck he is!
>
> **ALSO -2:**  **scocciatura** *f.* an annoying task, something that is a pain in the neck to do.
>
> **SYNONYM -1:**  **rompersi** *v.* • (lit.): to break oneself.
>
> **SYNONYM -2:**  **seccarsi** *v.* • (lit.): to dry oneself up.
>
> **SYNONYM -3:**  **stufarsi** *v.*
>
> > **NOTE:**  In its non-reflexive form, *stufare* means "to stew." Therefore, *stufarsi* could be loosely translated as "to stew oneself" which is a long, slow, and boring process.

**sentirsi giù** *exp.* to feel blah • (lit.): to feel down.

    *example:* **Mi sento giù** oggi. Penso di rimanere a casa a leggere.

    *translation:* I **feel blah** today. I think I'll just stay home and read.

    **SYNONYM:**     **sgasato/a** *adj.* • (lit.): from the verb *sgasarsi*, meaning "to let the gas out."


**sgranocchiare** *v.* to eat • (lit.): to munch, to nibble.

    *example:* Hai sempre fame? Ma se hai **sgranocchiato** tutto il giorno!

    *translation:* You're still hungry? You've been **eating** all day!


**vita (essere una)** *exp.* to be a long time • (lit.): to be a life(time).

    *example:* È **una vita** che non ti vedo! Come stai?

    *translation:* It's been **such a long time** since I've seen you! How are you?


# PRACTICE THE VOCABULARY

*(Answers to Lesson Nine, p. 188)*


## A. Underline the definition of the words in boldface.

1. **arrivare al capolinea**:
   a. to arrive in the nick of time
   b. to be at death's door

2. **carburare**:
   a. to hurry
   b. to feel well

3. **essere una vita**:
   a. to be a long time
   b. to see life throught rose-colored glasses

4. **sentirsi giù**:
   a. to feel blah
   b. to fall down

5. **essere in palla**:
   a. to be a bundle of nerves
   b. to be in tip-top shape

6. **scocciarsi**:
   a. to be having a blast
   b. to be bored

7. **da matti**:
   a. big-time
   b. to go crazy

8. **di nuovo**:
   a. brand-new
   b. again

9. **mah**:
   a. Mom
   b. so-so

10. **fare i gattini**:
    a. to sneeze
    b. to vomit

11. **la fine del mondo**:
    a. fantastic, awesome, out of this world
    b. the worst

12. **farsi una bevutina**:
    a. to have a drink
    b. to go to bed

## B. Complete the phrases below by choosing the appropriate words from the list.

| | |
|---|---|
| **CARBURO** | **SBOBA** |
| **OKAPPA** | **SCOCCIATO** |
| **MATTI** | **SGRANOCCHIATO** |
| **PALLA** | **TILT** |
| **PEZZI** | **VITA** |

1. – Ti piace la cioccolata?
   – Da _____!

2. Ero così preoccupato perchè eri in ritardo di due ore! Avevo lo stomaco a _____!

3. Mi sento in _____! Spero di non prendermi l'influenza!

4. Mi ero così _____ durante la lezione!

5. Hai assaggiato la _____ che Federica ha preparato ieri sera? Era tremenda!

6. È una _____ che non ti vedo! Come stai?

7. Hai sempre fame? Ma se hai _____tutto il giorno!

8. – Vuoi venire al cinema con me stasera?
   – _____, ma non posso fare tardi perchè devo cominciare a lavorare presto domattina.

9. Sono stato male per una settimana, ma ora sono nuovamente in _____!

10. Non _____. Penso che dovrei andare a casa e mettermi a letto.

## C. Match the English phrase in the left column with the Italian translation from the right. Write the appropriate letter in the box.

☐ 1. I'm tired of being **cooped up** in the house all day.

A. Sono **scocciato**! Che orribile festa!

☐ 2. Lucia has **a ton of** plants in her house.

B. Lucia ha **un macello** di piante a casa sua.

☐ 3. Every time I go on a boat, I **barf**.

C. Sono stanco di starmene **ibernato** in casa tutto il giorno.

☐ 4. Would you like to go **get a drink** before we go to the movie?

D. **Mi sento giù** oggi. Spero di non ammalarmi.

☐ 5. If you're not successful the first time, try **again**!

E. Vogliamo andare a **farci una bevutina** prima di andare al cine?

☐ 6. – How are you doing today?
– **So-so**. Last week I actually felt better.

F. Tutte le volte che vado in barca, **faccio i gattini**.

☐ 7. **I'm bored**. What a horrible party!

G. – Come ti senti oggi?
– **Mah**. Stavo meglio la settimana scorsa.

☐ 8. My stomach **was in knots** waiting to hear whether I got the job.

H. Avevo lo stomaco **a pezzi** mentre aspettavo di sapere se mi avevano assunto.

☐ 9. **I feel blah** today. I hope I'm not getting sick.

I. Se non ci riesci la prima volta, prova **di nuovo**!

☐ 10. You're still hungry? You've been **eating** all day!

J. Hai sempre fame? Ma se hai **sgranocchiato** tutto il giorno!

## D. FIND-A-WORD CUBE
**Using the list below, circle the words in the cube on page 151 that are missing from the dialogue below. Words may be spelled horizontally or vertically.**

| | | |
|---|---|---|
| **BEVUTINA** | **IBERNATO** | **PEZZI** |
| **BUSCATO** | **IMPIOMBATI** | **SBOBA** |
| **CAPOLINEA** | **MATTI** | **SCOCCIATO** |
| **CARBURATO** | **MONDO** | **SGRANOCCHIARE** |
| **GATTINI** | **NUOVO** | **TILT** |
| **GIÙ** | **OKAPPA** | **VITA** |

*Federico:*  Come va? **È una** _____ che non ci vediamo! Stai

bene?

*Paolo:*  **Mah**. **Non ho** _____ per una settimana. All'inizio

**mi sentivo soltanto un po'** _____, poi le cose sono

peggiorate. Ho capito di essermi _____ l'influenza e

allora sono **andato in** _____. Ho avuto un maledetto

mal di testa, il mio stomaco era **a** _____, e per poco non

ho **fatto i** _____. Ho avuto quasi l'impressione di

essere **arrivato al** _____.

*Federico:*   Mi dispiace, ma sono felice di vederti **in palla di**

        _____ .

*Paolo:*   Figurati! **Mi ero così** _____ a starmene

        _____ in casa tutta la settimana.

*Federico:*   Ho un'idea. Andiamoci a vedere un film al cinema qui dietro

        l'angolo. Ci divertiremo un casino! Quel film deve essere **la fine**

        **del** _____ .

*Paolo:*   _____! Spero soltanto che non sia uno di quei film

        dove tutti finiscono _____ . Ma le commedie mi

        piacciono **da** _____!

*Federico:*   Anche a me. Poi, dopo il film possiamo andare al ritrovo qui

        vicino, a **farci una** _____ . Ti consiglio

        comunque di non prenderci niente da _____ ,

        perchè il cibo lì è davvero una _____ .

# FIND-A- WORD CUBE

# E. DICTATION
## Test Your Listening Comprehension

*(This dictation can be found in the Appendix on page 197.)*

If you are following along with your cassette, you will now hear a series of sentences from the opening dialogue. These sentences will be read by a native speaker at normal conversational speed (which may seem fast to you at first). In addition, the words will be pronounced as you would actually hear them in a conversation, often including some common reductions.

The first time the sentences are presented, simply listen in order to get accustomed to the speed and heavy use of reductions. The sentences will then be read again with a pause after each to give you time to write down what you heard. The third time the sentences are read, follow along with what you have written.

# Mamma mia! Che *tappo grasso!*

(trans.): Wow! What a **fat slob**!
(lit.): My mother! What a **fat cork**!

# LEZIONE DIECI · Dialogue in Slang

*Elena:* Questo ristorante ti piacerà molto. Il cibo qui è **megagalattico**! Ed è anche un posticino così romatico se vuoi **metterti** con qualcuno.

*Stefania:* Veramente sono già stata qui. È stata la serata più brutta della mia vita.

*Elena:* E perchè? Che è successo?

*Stefania:* Sono uscita con uno che lavora con me. Forse lo conosci; si chiama Matteo De Lucia. Lui è quel **tappo grasso** che gira sempre con un berretto in testa. Quando l'ho conosciuto la prima volta, ho pensato che fosse davvero **super bono**. Ma quando abbiamo finito di cenare, mi sono resa conto che era soltanto un **rompi scatole**! Per prima cosa, ha **buttato giù tutto come un lavandino**. Avresti dovuto vedere come ha buttato giù quel cibo! Poi si è **incavolato** con il **buttafuori**, sono **venuti alle mani**, e alla fine gli ha **allungato un dritto** nel **becco**!

*Elena:* Questo è semplicemente **osceno**! Doveva essere o **ubriaco fradicio** o magari un po'**partito**.

*Stefania:* Ma c'è di più. Il tutto si è trasformato in un vero **bordello**. Sono arrivati gli **sbirri** per arrestarlo e portarlo via con i **ferri**. Sono sicura che un po'di **gabbia** lo aiuterà a **sgasarsi**.

# Wow!
# What a *fat slob*

Elena: You're going to love this restaurant. The food here is **big-time awesome**! And it's such a romantic place if you're **beginning a relationship** with someone.

Stefania: I've actually been here before. It was the worst night of my entire life.

Elena: Why? What happened?

Stefania: I went out with a guy from work. You may know him; his name is Matteo De Lucia. He's the **short, fat guy** who always wears a cap. When I first met him, I thought he was really **gorgeous**. But after dinner, I realized that he was nothing but a **pain in the neck**! First of all, he **eats like a pig**. You should have seen the way he downed his food! Then he **flew off the handle** with the **bouncer**, **got into a fight**, and **punched him** in the **mouth**!

Elena: That's simply **outrageous**! He must have either been **roaring drunk** or simply **lost touch with reality**.

Stefania: But there's more. Everything turned into total **chaos**. The **cops** came to arrest him and took him away in **handcuffs**. I'm sure that a little time in the **slammer** will make him **come off his high horse**.

# My mother!
# What a *fat cork!*

*Elena:*     You're going to love this restaurant. The food here is
**mega-galactic**! And it's such a romantic place if you're
**putting yourself** with someone.

*Stefania:*  I've actually been here before. It was the worst night of my entire
life.

*Elena:*     Why? What happened?

*Stefania:*  I went out with a guy who works with me. You may know him;
his name is Matteo De Lucia. He's the **fat cork** who always
wears a cap. When I first met him, I thought he was really **super
good**. But after dinner I realized that he was nothing but a
**box-breaker**! First of all, he **throws down everything as
if he were a sink**. You should have seen the way he downed
his food! Then he **threw himself in the cabbage** with the
**"thrower-outter," came to hands**, and **extended him a
straight one** in the **beak**!

*Elena:*     That's simply **obscene**! He must have either been **soaking
wet drunk** or simply **gone**.

*Stefania:*  And there's more. Everything turned into a real **brothel**. The
**men in hoods** came to arrest him and took him away in
**irons**. I'm sure that a little **cage** will make him **let his gas
out**.

# VOCABULARY

**allungare un dritto** *exp.* to give someone a direct punch, to punch someone dead on • (lit.): to extend a straight.

> *example:* Quando ho detto a Matteo che non mi piaceva la sua macchina nuova, lui mi ha **allungato un dritto**!
>
> *translation:* When I told Matteo that I didn't like his new car, he **punched** me!

**becco** *m.* mouth • (lit.): beak.

> *example:* Chiudi il **becco**! Non dici altro che bugie!
>
> *translation:* Shut your **mouth**! All you ever do is lie!

**bordello** *m.* uproar, hubbub • (lit.): brothel.

> *example:* Che **bordello** c'è là fuori? Sembra che qualcuno se le stia dando!
>
> *translation:* What's the **uproar** outside? It sounds like someone is having a fight!
>
> **SYNONYM -1:** **baccano** *m.* • (lit.): from Bacchus (the Greek god of parties).
>
> **SYNONYM -2:** **caciara** *f.*
>
> **SYNONYM -3:** **cagnara** *f.*
>
> **SYNONYM -4:** **casino** *m.* • (lit.): brothel.
>
> **SYNONYM -5:** **chiasso** *m.*
>
> **SYNONYM -6:** **fracasso** *m.*
>
> **SYNONYM -7:** **gazzarra** *f.*

**buttafuori** *m.* bouncer (in a bar, hotel, etc.) • (lit.): from *buttare,* meaning "to throw," and *fuori,* meaning "out."

> *example:* Ieri sera Francesco era così ubriaco e rumoroso che il **buttafuori** lo ha cacciato!
>
> *translation:* Last night, Francesco got so drunk and loud that the **bouncer** threw him out!
>
> **ANTONYM:** **buttadentro** *m.* the bouncer who greets people at the door and allows only those who are authorized to enter • (lit.): the "throw inside."

**buttare giù tutto come un lavandino** *exp.* to eat like a pig •
(lit.): to thrown down everything as if one were a sink.

> *example:* Maria **butta giù tutto come un lavandino**, ma
> ciò nonostante è sempre magra!
>
> *translation:* Maria **eats like she has a hollow leg**, but she's still
> so thin!

**ferri** *m.pl.* handcuffs • (lit.): irons.

> *example:* Ho appena visto la polizia portare Marcello con i **ferri**!
> Chissà cosa ha fatto!
>
> *translation:* I just saw Marcello get taken away in **handcuffs** by
> the cops! I wonder what he did!

**gabbia** *f.* • **1.** jail, "slammer" • **2.** loony bin • (lit.): cage.

> *example:* Il fratelo di Stefania starà in **gabbia** per un anno per
> aver guidato in stato di ebbrezza!
>
> *translation:* Stefania's brother is going to be in the **slammer** for a
> year for drunk driving!

> **SYNONYM -1:** **al fresco** *m.* (as introduced in Lesson Three, p. 43) •
> (lit.): in the cool (as in, "to cool one's heels").

> **SYNONYM -2:** **essere dentro** *exp.* • (lit.): to be inside.

**incavolarsi** *v.* to fly off the handle, to get ticked off • (lit.): to throw
oneself in the cabbage (from *cavolo*, meaning "cabbage").

> *example:* **Mi sono incavolato** con mio fratello perchè ha
> preso la mia macchina senza chiedermela.
>
> *translation:* I **flew off the handle** with my brother because he
> borrowed my car without asking me.

> **SYNONYM:** **imbestialirsi** *v.* to become a *bestia*, meaning "beast."

**megagalattico** *adj.* big-time awesome, fantastic, super cool • (lit.):
mega-galactic.

> *example:* La casa di Elena è **megagalattica**! Ha addirittura una
> piscina in salotto!
>
> *translation:* Elena's house is **awesome**! She even has a swimming
> pool in her living room!

**NOTE:** The prefix *mega* can be added to the following single-word synonyms to add emphasis just as "super" or "big-time" does in English.

**SYNONYM -1:** **boreale** *adj.* (Northern Italy) • (lit.): borealis.

**SYNONYM -2:** **cosmico** *adj.* • (lit.): cosmic.

> **NOTE:** It's interesting to note that in the 1970s, the adjective *cosmic* was used in the United States to mean "fantastic."

**SYNONYM -3:** **fine del mondo** *exp.* • (lit.): the end of the world.

**SYNONYM -4:** **da flash** *exp.* (from English) • (lit.): from a flash or bulletin (such as a "newsflash").

**SYNONYM -5:** **mitico/a** *adj.* • (lit.): mythical, of mythic proportion.

**SYNONYM -6:** **mostruoso/a** *adj.* • (lit.): monstrous.

**SYNONYM -7:** **pazzesco/a** *adj.* (Northern & Central Italy) • (lit.): crazy, insane.

**SYNONYM -8:** **sano/a** *adj.* • (lit.): sane • It's interesting that in English, the opposite in slang applies: What an <u>in</u>sane car!

**SYNONYM -9:** **spaziale** *adj.* (as introduced in Lesson Three, p. 50) awesome, fantastic • (lit.): spacial.

**mettersi con qualcuno** *exp.* to begin a relationship with someone • (lit.): to put oneself with someone.

> *example:* Ho appena sentito che **ti sei messa con** Alfredo! È vero?
>
> *translation:* I just heard that you **started a relationship with** Alfredo! Is that true?

**osceno/a** *adj.* outrageous, extraordinary • (lit.): obscene.

> *example:* Stefania ha detto di aver trovato una scatola piena di soldi per strada? È **osceno**!
>
> *translation:* Stefania said she found a box full of money in the street? That's **outrageous**!

**partito/a** *adj.* lost touch with reality • (lit.): left (one's senses).

> *example:* Farai paracadutismo domani? Ma sei **partito**? È così pericoloso!
>
> *translation:* You're going to go skydiving tomorrow? Have you **lost it**? That's so dangerous!

**SYNONYM -1:**   **di fuori (essere)** *exp.* (as introduced in Lesson Two, p. 28) • (lit.): to be out (of one's mind).

**SYNONYM -2:**   **flippato/a** *adj.* (as introduced in Lesson Six, p. 99) • (lit.): flipped.

**SYNONYM -3:**   **fuori di testa (essere)** *exp.* (as introduced in Lesson Seven, p. 118) to be crazy • (lit.): to be out of one's head.

**SYNONYM -4:**   **girare** *v.* (Central Italy) • (lit.): to turn • *Ma ti gira il cervello?*; Are you nuts? (lit.): Is your brain turning?

**rompi scatole** *m.* annoying person, pain in the butt • (lit.): box-breaker.

     *example:*   Cecilia è così **rompi scatole**! Mi chiama la telefono tutte le volte che ha un problema!

     *translation:*   Cecilia is such a **pain in the butt**. She calls me on the phone every time she has a problem.

**NOTE:**   **scatole** *m.* butt • (lit.): box.

**SYNONYM -1:**   **borsa** *f.* • (lit.): bag.

**SYNONYM -2:**   **mattone** *m.* • (lit.): brick.

**SYNONYM -3:**   **menata** *f.* • annoying thing or situation (not applied to a person).

**SYNONYM -4:**   **palla** *f.* • **1.** an annoying person • **2.** a bore • (lit.): ball.

**SYNONYM -5:**   **rompimento/a** *n.* • (lit.): a breaker.

**sbirro** *m.* police officer, cop • (lit.): from Latin *birrum*, meaning "hooded cloak."

     *example:*   Corri a trovare uno **sbirro**! Credo che quell'uomo stia rapinando quella banca!

     *translation:*   Go run and find a **cop**! I think that man is robbing that bank!

**SYNONYM -1:**   **piedipiatti** *m.* • (lit.): flat feet.

**SYNONYM -2:**   **pula (la)** *f.* (as introduced in Lesson Three, p. 51) police officer, "cop" • (lit.): husk.

**sgasarsi** *v.* to come off one's high horse.

     *example:*   Luigi crede di essere troppo ganzo, ma non lo è. Lui deve cercare di **sgasarsi**!

     *translation:*   Luigi thinks he is way too cool, but he's not. He should try to **come off his high horse**!

**super bono/a** *adj.* super good-looking, gorgeous, hot • (lit.): super good.

    *example:* Marco è **super bono** ed io sono innamorata pazza di lui, ma purtroppo io non gli piaccio affatto.

    *translation:* Marco is **super hot** and I'm desperately in love with him, but unfortunately he doesn't like me at all.

**tappo grasso** *m.* short, fat guy • (lit.): fat cork.

    *example:* Davide e Alessio sono gemelli, ma Alessio è un gigante e Davide è un **tappo grasso**!

    *translation:* David and Alessio are twins, but Alessio is a giant and David is a **short, fat guy**!

**SYNONYM -1:** **ciccio bomba** *m.* • (lit.): fat bomb.

**SYNONYM -2:** **ciccione/a** *n.* fatty, tubby.

**ubriaco fradicio** *exp.* roaring drunk • (lit.): soaking wet drunk.

    *example:* Giovanni ha bevuto soltanto una birra ed è già **ubriaco fradicio**!

    *translation:* Giovanni only had one beer and he's already **roaring drunk**!

**SYNONYM -1:** **bere come una spugna** *exp.* to drink an excessive amount of alcohol • (lit.): to drink like a sponge.

**SYNONYM -2:** **bevuto/a** *adj.* • (lit.): the past tense of *bevere*, meaning "to drink."

**SYNONYM -3:** **inzupparsi** *v.* to get drunk • (lit.): to get soaked.

**venir alle mani** *exp.* to get into a fistfight, to come to blows • (lit.): to come to hands.

    *example:* Invece di risolvere il problema da persone mature, Ernesto e Simone sono **venuti alle mani** per una stupidaggine!

    *translation:* Instead of having a mature discussion, Ernesto and Simone **got into a fistfight** over something really stupid!

**SYNONYM -1:** **fare a cazzotti** *exp.* • (lit.): to do punches.

**SYNONYM -2:** **piallare** *v.* to flatten someone • (lit.): to plane.

# PRACTICE THE VOCABULARY

*(Answers to Lesson Ten, p. 190)*

## A. Fill in the blanks with the word that best completes the phrase.

BECCO               GABBIA
BORDELLO            INCAVOLATO
DRITTO              SBIRRO
FERRI               SCATOLE
FRADICIO            TAPPO

1. Cecilia è così rompi _____! Mi chiama al telefono tutte le volte che ha un problema!

2. Giovanni ha bevuto soltanto una birra ed è già ubriaco _____!

3. Il fratello di Stefania starà in _____ per un anno per aver guidato in stato di ebbrezza.

4. Ho appena visto la polizia portare Marcello con i _____! Chissà cosa ha fatto!?

5. Mi sono _____ con mio fratello perchè ha preso la mia macchina senza chiedermela.

6. Quando ho detto a Matteo che non mi piaceva la sua macchina nuova, lui mi ha allungato un _____!

7. Che _____ c'è là fuori? Sembra che qualcuno se le stia dando!

8. Corri a trovare uno _____! Credo che quell'uomo stia rapinando quella banca!

9. Davide e Alessio sono gemelli, ma Alessio è un gigante e Davide è un _____ grasso!

10. Chiudi il _____! Non dici altro che bugie!

# B. Underline the definition of the words in boldface.

1. **becco**:
   a. boot
   b. mouth

2. **allungare un dritto**:
   a. to go to bed
   b. to punch someone dead on

3. **tappo grasso**:
   a. a genius
   b. a short, fat guy

4. **venir alle mani**:
   a. to get into a fistfight
   b. to arrive to work

5. **rompi scatole**:
   a. an annoying person
   b. one who is prone to accidents

6. **sbirro**:
   a. a police officer, cop
   b. an old car

7. **osceno**:
   a. outrageous, extraordinary
   b. smelly

8. **partito**:
   a. lost touch with reality
   b. extremely intelligent

9. **ferri**:
   a. a small boat
   b. handcuffs

10. **megagalattico**:
    a. big-time awesome, fantastic
    b. extremely fat

11. **gabbia**:
    a. one who talks nonstop
    b. jail, "slammer"

12. **mettersi con qualcuno**:
    a. to begin a relationship with someone
    b. to go out with someone

13. **buttare giù tutto come un lavandino**:
    a. to leave in a hurry
    b. to eat like a pig

14. **incavolarsi**:
    a. to fly off the handle, to get ticked off
    b. to sleep

15. **sgasarsi**:
    a. to come off one's high horse
    b. to laugh

16. **buttafuori**:
    a. a bouncer
    b. a fast car

## C. Underline the word that best completes the phrase.

1. Che (**baccello**, **bordello**, **anello**)! Chissà cosa sta succedendo là fuori!

2. Quando Fabrizio mi ha insultato, mi sono arrabbiato così tanto che gli ho allungato un (**dritto**, **fritto**, **ardito**).

3. Giovanni era un atleta una volta. Non riesco a credere che sia diventato un (**topo**, **acchiappo**, **tappo**) grasso!

4. Non puoi guidare! Sei ubriaco (**sudicio**, **fradicio**, **pratico**)!

5. Dopo essersi insultati per un'ora, Gabriele e Francesco, alla fine, sono venuti alle (**mani**, **pani**, **mini**)!

6. Il mio fratellino mi segue da tutte le parti. È veramente un rompi (**setole**, **botole**, **scatole**)!

7. Mi hanno appena rubato la macchina! Svelto! Va' a cercare uno (**sbirro**, **biro**, **subito**)!

8. Guarda quanta bella roba da mangiare! Ho in mente di buttare giù tutto come un (**lavorino**, **biondino**, **lavandino**).

9. Hanno appena portato via quel tipo con i (**panni**, **ferri**, **neri**). Chissà cos'ha fatto di male.

10. Mi sono (**incavolato**, **cavolino**, **volato**) quando sono uscito dal supermercato e ho visto che qualcuno mi aveva ammaccato la macchina!

11. La tua nuova casa è (**megagalattica**, **lattica**, **attica**)! Congratulazioni!

12. Scierai giù da quella collina all'indietro? Ma sei (**pagano**, **partito**, **pulito**)? Ti ammazzerai!

## D. CROSSWORD
### Fill in the crossword puzzle on page 167 by choosing the correct word(s) from the list below.

| | | |
|---|---|---|
| **BECCO** | **GABBIA** | **SBIRRO** |
| **BORDELLO** | **INCAVOLARSI** | **SCATOLE** |
| **BUTTAFUORI** | **MANI** | **SGASARSI** |
| **BUTTARE** | **MEGAGALATICCO** | **SUPER** |
| **DRITTO** | **METTERSI** | **TAPPO** |
| **FERRI** | **OSCENO** | |
| **FRADICIO** | **PARTITO** | |

## ACROSS

5. \_\_\_\_ *f.* • **1.** jail, "slammer" • **2.** looney bin • (lit.): cage.

20. \_\_\_\_ *m.* uproar, hubbub • (lit.): brothel.

24. \_\_\_\_ **grasso** *m.* short, fat guy • (lit.): fat cork.

25. \_\_\_\_ *v.* to come off one's high horse.

36. \_\_\_\_ *m.* bouncer (in a bar, hotel, etc.) • (lit.): from *buttare*, meaning "to throw," and *fuori*, meaning "out."

41. \_\_\_\_ **con qualcuno** *v.* to begin a relationship with someone • (lit.): to put oneself with someone.

47. \_\_\_\_ *v.* to fly off the handle, to get ticked off • (lit.): to be in the cabbage (from *cavolo*, meaning "cabbage").

55. **venir alle** \_\_\_\_\_ *exp.* to get into a fistfight, to come to blows • (lit.): to come to hands.

61. **allungare un** \_\_\_\_ *exp.* to give someone a direct punch, to punch someone dead on • (lit.): to extend a straight.

# DOWN

3. \_\_\_\_ **bono/a** *adj.* super good-looking, gorgeous • (lit.): super good.

7. \_\_\_\_ *m.* mouth • (lit.): beak.

11. \_\_\_\_ *m.* police officer, cop • (lit.): from Latin *birrum,* meaning "hooded cloak."

17. \_\_\_\_ *adj.* lost touch with reality • (lit.): left (one's senses).

19. \_\_\_\_ *adj.* big-time awesome, fantastic, super cool • (lit.): mega galactic.

36. \_\_\_\_ giù tutto come un lavandino *exp.* to eat like a pig • (lit.): to thrown down everything as if one were a sink.

39. \_\_\_\_ *m.pl.* handcuffs • (lit.): irons.

48. \_\_\_\_ *adj.* outrageous, extraordinary • (lit.): obscene.

49. **rompi** \_\_\_\_ *m.* annoying person, pain in the butt • (lit.): box breaker.

# CROSSWORD PUZZLE

# E. DICTATION
## Test Your Listening Comprehension

*(This dictation can be found in the Appendix on page 197.)*

If you are following along with your cassette, you will now hear a series of sentences from the opening dialogue. These sentences will be read by a native speaker at normal conversational speed (which may seem fast to you at first). In addition, the words will be pronounced as you would actually hear them in a conversation, often including some common reductions.

The first time the sentences are presented, simply listen in order to get accustomed to the speed and heavy use of reductions. The sentences will then be read again with a pause after each to give you time to write down what you heard. The third time the sentences are read, follow along with what you have written.

# REVIEW EXAM FOR LESSONS 6-10

*(Answers to Review, p. 191)*

## A. Choose the correct definition of the words in boldface. Circle your answer.

1. [fra noi,] **a quattr'occhi**:
   a. just between you and me
   b. someone who wears glasses, "four-eyes"

2. **allocco**:
   a. genius
   b. numbskull, idiot

3. **allungare un dritto**:
   a. to go to bed
   b. to punch someone dead on

4. **arrivare al capolinea**:
   a. to arrive in the nick of time
   b. to be at death's door

5. **becco**:
   a. boot
   b. mouth

6. **buttafuori**:
   a. bouncer
   b. fast car

7. **buttare giù tutto come un lavandino**:
   a. to leave in a hurry
   b. to eat like a pig

8. **carburare**:
   a. to hurry
   b. to feel well

9. **cariatide**:
   a. deadweight (said of a person)
   b. a person who is very uptight

10. **cincischiare**:
    a. to eat
    b. to waste time doing nothing productive

11. **ciucco**:
    a. crazy
    b. drunk

12. **da matti**:
    a. big-time
    b. to go crazy

13. **dare una ripassata a qualcuno**:
    a. to reprimand someone
    b. to give someone a black eye

14. **di nuovo**:
    a. brand new
    b. again

15. **essere in palla**:
    a. to be a bundle of nerves
    b. to be in tip-top shape

16. **essere una vita**:
    a. to be a long time
    b. to see life throught rose-colored glasses

17. **fare i gattini**:
    a. to cough
    b. to vomit

18. **fare una soffiata**:
    a. to report someone, to be a snitch
    b. to take a nap

19. **farsi il culo**:
    a. to work extremely hard
    b. to talk nonstop

20. **farsi una bevutina**:
    a. to have a drink
    b. to go to bed

21. **fasullo**:
    a. fake, faker
    b. exceptionally tall woman

22. **ferri**:
    a. small boat
    b. handcuffs

23. **fesso**:
    a. genius
    b. stupid

24. **fregatura**:
    a. fracture
    b. thievery, rip-off

25. **fuori di testa (essere)**:
    a. to be excited, thrilled
    b. to be crazy

26. **gabbia**:
    a. one who talks nonstop
    b. jail, "slammer"

27. **in gamba (essere)**:
    a. to run quickly
    b. to be on the ball

28. **incavolarsi**:
    a. to fly off the handle, to get ticked off
    b. to sleep

29. **intoppare qualcuno**:
    a. to kill someone
    b. to see someone unexpectedly

30. **la fine del mondo**:
    a. fantastic, awesome, out of this world
    b. the worst

## B. Fill in the blanks with the word that best completes the phrase.

| | | |
|---|---|---|
| **BECCO** | **MATTI** | **TAPPO** |
| **BIRRA** | **PIOVE** | **TILT** |
| **CARBURO** | **QUATTR'OCCHI** | **TIRA** |
| **DRITTO** | **SCATOLE** | **VITA** |

1. Cecilia è così rompi _____! Mi chiama la telefono tutte le volte che ha un problema!

2. Quando ho detto a Matteo che non mi piaceva la sua macchina nuova, lui mi ha allungato un _____!

3. Davide e Alessio sono gemelli, ma Alessio è un gigante e Davide è un _____ grasso!

4. Chiudi il _____! Non dici altro che bugie!

5. – Ti piace la cioccolata?
   – Da _____!

6. È una _____ che non ti vedo! Come stai?

7. Non _____. Penso che dovrei andare a casa e mettermi a letto.

8. Sono stato bene per una settimana, ma ora sono nuovamente in _____!

9. Dobbiamo metterci a lavorare a tutta _____, se vogliamo finire questo lavoro per le 5:00!

10. Fra noi, a _____, ho saputo che Sergio vede un'altra donna all'insaputa di sua moglie.

11. Il capo ha appena chiamato Pasquale nel suo ufficio. Scommetto che lo licenzierà. Non ci _____!

12. Niente mi _____ in questo negozio. Andiamo da qualche altra parte.

## C. Match the English phrase in the left column with the Italian translation from the right. Write the appropriate letter in the box.

1. Cinzia used to be so pretty but now she's a real **troll**! I wonder what happened to her!

2. Did you see the price on that jacket? What a rip-off!

3. Matteo is a **short, fat guy**, but his wife is tall and slender.

4. Would you like me to give you a lift to the market?

5. You're going out with Mariella? Are you **out of your mind**? She already has a boyfriend who is the biggest guy in school!

6. When my grandparents came to this country, they **didn't have a red cent**. Now they own a successful business.

7. Did you see the **ugly clothes** Chiara was wearing in school? She looked terrible!

8. This liquor is **disgustingly** strong!

9. Luigi dyed his hair orange? Oh, brother!

10. Don't go see that movie! I saw it yesterday and it was a real **bore**!

A. Esci con Mariella? Ma sei **fuori di testa**? Lei ha già un ragazzo, per giunta il più grosso della scuola!

B. Hai visto il prezzo su quella giacca? Che **fregatura**!

C. Hai visto che **stracci** aveva addosso Chiara a scuola? Stava malissimo!

D. Matteo è un **barilotto**, mentre sua moglie è alta e snella.

E. Cinzia era così carina, e ora è una **scorfana**! Chissà che le è successo!

F. Quando i miei nonni sono arrivati in questo paese, non avevano il **becco d'un quattrino**. Ora invece sono proprietari di un bel negozio!

G. Questo liquore è forte **da fare schifo**!

H. Non andare a vedere quel film! L'ho visto ieri ed era una tale **pizza**!

I. Vuoi che ti dia uno **strappo** al mercato?

J. Luigi si è tinto i capelli d'arancione? **Buona notte**!

# D. Underline the word that best completes the phrase.

1. Dopo essersi insultati per un'ora, Gabriele e Francesco, alla fine, sono venuti alle (**mani**, **pani**, **mini**)!

2. Guarda quanta bella roba da mangiare! Ho in mente di buttare giù tutto come un (**lavorino**, **biondino**, **lavandino**).

3. Lavoro a tutta (**birra**, **bara**, **sbirro**) da due settimane per finire in tempo.

4. Il mio fratellino mi segue da tutte le parti. È veramente un rompi (**setole**, **botole**, **scatole**)!

5. Ho creduto a Marco, ma lui mi ha preso in (**giostra**, **giro**, **ghiro**).

6. Mi piace un sacco Giorgio. È proprio una (**pizza**, **palla**, **pasta**) d'uomo.

7. Carlotta è di nuovo in ospedale? Pensavo che stesse meglio. Sono rimasto così sorpreso quando ho saputo che perdeva (**colpi**, **calci**, **corpi**).

8. Mi hanno appena rubato la macchina! Svelto! Va' a cercare uno (**sbirro**, **biro**, **subito**)!

9. Non mi sono divertito affatto a lezione. Era davvero una (**pizza**, **pazza**, **pozza**)

10. Dovresti vedere che casa ha appena comprato Matteo. È enorme! Deve essere ricco (**sfondato**, **fidanzato**, **sfasato**).

11. La mia vicina di casa parla sempre da sola. Credo che sia (**flippata**, **flipperata**, **fulminata**).

12. È difficile ascoltare il film, perchè la donna dietro di noi parla in continuazione. Le dico di (**chinarsi**, **chetarsi**, **chiacchierare**).

# ANSWERS TO LESSONS 1-10

## LEZIONE UNO – *Per la terza volta questa settimana, Antonio ha fatto forca a scuola!*
*(For the third time this week, Antonio cut class!)*

### PRACTICE THE VOCABULARY

A. 1. casino
   2. beccato
   3. meningi
   4. scartoffie
   5. forca
   6. l'ultima
   7. vecchi
   8. sega
   9. protetta
   10. ruffiano

B. 1. bonazza
   2. cavolo
   3. fuori
   4. sgobbare
   5. sega
   6. scazzato
   7. castagna
   8. buco
   9. becca
   10. ruffiana

C. 1. E
   2. G
   3. A
   4. J
   5. D
   6. F
   7. H
   8. B
   9. C
   10. I

D. **CROSSWORD PUZZLE**

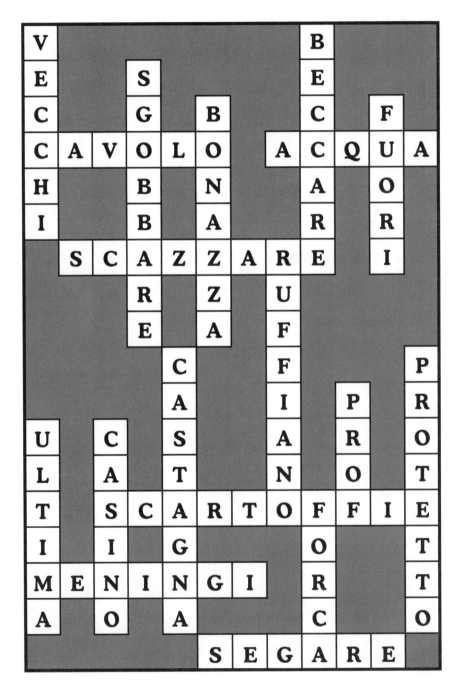

## LEZIONE DUE – *Francesca ha una cotta per Giovanni!*
*(Francesca has a crush on Giovanni!)*

### PRACTICE THE VOCABULARY

A.  1. C
    2. A
    3. H
    4. B
    5. E
    6. G
    7. D
    8. F

B.  1. bomba
    2. notte
    3. succhiotto
    4. bottega
    5. tipo
    6. tirato
    7. palla
    8. seminato
    9. lanciarmi
    10. cotta

C.  1. a
    2. b
    3. b
    4. b
    5. a
    6. a
    7. a
    8. a
    9. a
    10. b
    11. a
    12. b
    13. a
    14. a
    15. a
    16. a
    17. b
    18. b

## D. **DIALOGUE**

*Simona:*    Dove vai, così tutta **tirata**? Che fai? Esci con un **tipo** nuovo?

*Francesca:*    Lui non è certamente il mio ragazzo! Vado a cena fuori con Marco Papini.

*Simona:*    Vuoi dire con quel **lungagnone** che si mette sempre quei **cenci** larghi addosso? È un **secchionaccio della madonna**! Ieri in classe ha fatto questa noiosissima presentazione, e per tutto il tempo **aveva la bottega aperta**. Sono **morta** dalle risate! Non mi dire che **hai una bella cotta per quello**!

*Francesca:*    Eh, sì, **buona notte**! Tutte le volte che lo vedo avvicinarsi a me, cerco di **seminarlo**, ma lui mi blocca sempre. Mi ha **scocciato** per un mese chiedendomi di uscire, così alla fine gli ho detto di sì. Stasera sarà una **palla** indescrivibile.

*Simona:*    Di solito lui è così teso. Mi sorprende che questa volta abbia avuto il coraggio di **lanciarsi**. Forse questa volta riuscirà a convincerti!

*Francesca:*    Ma tu sei **di fuori**!

*Simona:*    Forse, ma se ti vedo tornare con un **succhiotto** al collo, vuol dire che la vostra serata è stata una **bomba**!

*Francesca:*    Ha, ha, molto spiritosa! Che fortuna se mi **tirasse un bidone**!


# LEZIONE TRE – *Pasquale si è spennato a forza di fare sempre benzina!*

*(Pasquale went broke buying gas all the time!)*

## PRACTICE THE VOCABULARY

A.   1.  bomba                6.  scheggi

     2.  spappolava         7.  carcassa

     3.  sassate              8.  spennato

     4.  strappo              9.  succhia

     5.  spaziale           10.  fresco

B.  1. I
    2. C
    3. F
    4. A
    5. E

    6. G
    7. B
    8. D
    9. H
    10. J

## C. CROSSWORD PUZZLE

D.  1. kaput
    2. Ammazza
    3. spennato
    4. strappo
    5. pula

    6. Spaziale
    7. babbiona
    8. culo
    9. spappolati
    10. scheggiare

## LEZIONE QUATTRO – *Il mio ospite comincia a starmi sull'anima!*

*(My houseguest is starting to get on my nerves!)*

### PRACTICE THE VOCABULARY

A.    1. a          7. a
       2. b          8. a
       3. b          9. a
       4. a        10. a
       5. b        11. b
       6. a        12. b

B.   **FIND-A-WORD PUZZLE**

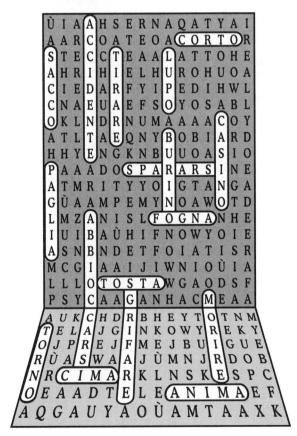

C.  1. C       6. A
    2. F       7. I
    3. H       8. B
    4. E       9. J
    5. G      10. D

D.  1. c       8. a
    2. b       9. a
    3. a      10. b
    4. a      11. c
    5. c      12. b
    6. b      13. c
    7. c      14. b

# LEZIONE CINQUE – *Come fa uno a vivere in una tale topaia?*

*(How can anyone live in such a rattrap?)*

## PRACTICE THE VOCABULARY

A.  1. palle       6. filiamocela
    2. maiale       7. topaia
    3. grande       8. buzzino
    4. trampoli       9. ciospa
    5. barche      10. balena

B.  1. rapa       7. pieno
    2. ciospa       8. culo
    3. palle       9. buzzino
    4. trampoli      10. maiale
    5. stronzo      11. diavolo
    6. figata      12. barche

C.  1.  B                                    6.  J
    2.  C                                    7.  G
    3.  F                                    8.  A
    4.  I                                    9.  H
    5.  E                                   10.  D


D.  **DIALOGUE**

*Alessandra:*   Ciao, Alberto e Chiara!  Vi state divertendo al mio **party**?

*Alberto:*      Oh, sì!  **Alla grande**!  È una gran **figata**!

                *[Poi, quando Alessandra si allontana...]*

                **Che palle**!  Stento a credere che lei riesca a vivere in questa **topaia**!  Ascolta, **ho fatto il pieno**!  **Filiamocela**!

*Chiara:*       Siamo appena arrivati!  Oh, no.  Vedi quel **buzzino** con quel paio di vecchie **barche** ai piedi?  Si chiama Roberto Ferri.  Spero che non mi veda!  Lui mi **sta davvero sul culo**.  Quello **stronzo ci prova** tutte le volte con me.  Continuo a **mandarlo al diavolo** ma quella **testa di rapa** non demorde e insiste a voler uscire con me.  Ti assicuro che se è per me lui continuerà ad **andare in bianco**.  Chi è quella **ciospa** con quei **trampoli** che gli sta vicino?

*Alberto:*      Oh, quella è Annamaria Corsi.  Lei è diventata davvero una **balena**!

*Chiara:*       Non mi sorprende.  Guarda come **si abbuffa come un maiale**!

# ANSWERS TO REVIEW EXAM 1-5

A.
| | | |
|---|---|---|
| 1. a | 11. b | 21. b |
| 2. b | 12. a | 22. a |
| 3. b | 13. b | 23. a |
| 4. a | 14. a | 24. a |
| 5. b | 15. a | 25. a |
| 6. a | 16. b | 26. b |
| 7. a | 17. a | 27. a |
| 8. b | 18. a | 28. a |
| 9. b | 19. a | 29. a |
| 10. a | 20. b | 30. b |

B.
| | |
|---|---|
| 1. sgobbare | 6. lanciarmi |
| 2. buco | 7. spaziale |
| 3. bomba | 8. spennato |
| 4. bottega | 9. maiale |
| 5. fuori | 10. sassate |

C.
| | |
|---|---|
| 1. F | 6. G |
| 2. H | 7. C |
| 3. A | 8. I |
| 4. J | 9. E |
| 5. B | 10. D |

D.
1. ciospa
2. figata
3. buzzino
4. diavolo
5. Ammazza
6. kaput
7. strappo
8. spappolati
9. sega
10. l'ultima
11. protetta
12. forca

## LEZIONE SEI – *Il mio vicino è flippato e dovrebbe andare da uno strizzacervelli!*

*(My neighbor's nuts and should go see a shrink!)*

### PRACTICE THE VOCABULARY

A. **CROSSWORD PUZZLE**

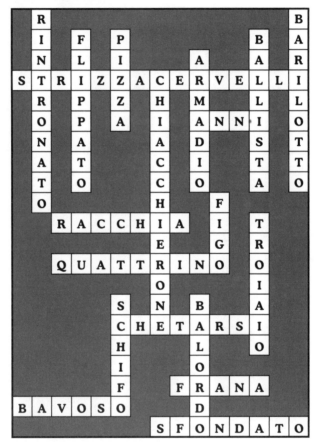

B.
1. armadio
2. bavoso
3. troiaio
4. strizzacervelli
5. rintronato

6. chiacchierone
7. flippato
8. figo
9. becco d'un quattrino
10. schifo

C.  1. ballista
    2. porta
    3. racchia
    4. barilotto
    5. becco
    6. figo
    7. chiacchierona
    8. pizza
    9. sfondato
    10. flippata
    11. chetarsi
    12. troiaio

D.  1. C
    2. A
    3. F
    4. I
    5. B
    6. G
    7. H
    8. D
    9. J
    10. E

# LEZIONE SETTE – *Graziella è davvero diventata una scorfana!*

*(Graziella has really turned into a troll!)*

## PRACTICE THE VOCABULARY

A.  1. b          7. b
    2. b          8. a
    3. a          9. a
    4. a          10. a
    5. b          11. b
    6. b          12. a

B.
1. tira
2. sputtanato
3. sacchi
4. fregatura
5. pappare

6. sbraco
7. scoppiata
8. intoppato
9. balenottera
10. scorfana

C. **FIND-A-WORD PUZZLE**

D.
1. D
2. F
3. B
4. G
5. E

6. H
7. C
8. I
9. A
10. J

## **LEZIONE OTTO** – *Pensavo che Oreste fosse una pasta d'uomo.*

*(I've used to think Oreste was a good egg.)*

### **PRACTICE THE VOCABULARY**

A.  1.  a
    2.  a
    3.  b
    4.  b
    5.  a
    6.  a
    7.  a
    8.  a
    9.  a
    10.  b
    11.  b
    12.  b
    13.  b
    14.  a
    15.  a

B.  1.  birra
    2.  giro
    3.  fico
    4.  gamba
    5.  quattr'occhi
    6.  capoccia
    7.  piove
    8.  ripassata
    9.  culo
    10.  cariatide

C.  1.  occhi
    2.  cariatide
    3.  capoccia
    4.  birra
    5.  giro
    6.  pasta
    7.  colpi
    8.  fesso
    9.  piove
    10.  fico
    11.  ripassata
    12.  culo

D. **DIALOGUE**

*Luigi:*    Hai sentito che è successo a Oreste Santovini?

*Sergio:*   Vuoi dire il nuovo impiegato? No, che gli è successo?

*Luigi:*    Fra noi, **a quattr'occhi**, credo che sarà licenziato. Su questo
            **non ci piove**.

*Sergio:*   E perchè?

*Luigi:*    Quando l'ho visto la prima volta, ho pensato che fosse una
            **pasta d'uomo** e veramente **in gamba** nel suo lavoro. I primi
            due giorni ha lavorato **a tutta birra**, poi ha cominciato a
            **perdere colpi** e ora sembra soltanto una **cariatide**.
            **Cincischia** e **non fa un fico** tutto il giorno. Sono io quello
            che deve **farsi il culo** perchè io finisco per fare anche il suo!

*Sergio:*   Ha veramente **preso in giro** il capo. Mi sorprende che sia
            stato così **fesso**. A dire il vero fin dal primo momento ho
            pensato che fosse un po'**fasullo**.

*Luigi:*    Il **capoccia gli ha dato una ripassata** perchè qualcuno gli
            ha **fatto una soffiata** che Oreste veniva a **sfacchinare**
            completamente **ciucco**!

# LEZIONE NOVE – *Paolo si è sentito a pezzi ieri.*
*(Paolo was exhausted yesterday.)*

## PRACTICE THE VOCABULARY

A.  1. b               5. b               9. b
    2. b               6. b              10. b
    3. a               7. a              11. a
    4. a               8. b              12. a

B.
1. matti
2. pezzi
3. tilt
4. scocciato
5. sboba
6. vita
7. sgranocchiato
8. okappa
9. palla
10. carburo

C.
1. C
2. B
3. F
4. E
5. I
6. G
7. A
8. H
9. D
10. J

D.  **FIND-A-WORD CUBE**

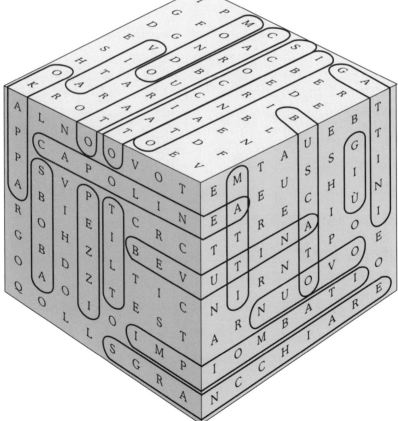

# LEZIONE DIECI – *Mamma mia!*
## *Che tappo grasso!*

*(Wow! What a fat slob!)*

## PRACTICE THE VOCABULARY

A.   1.  scatole
    2.  fradicio
    3.  gabbia
    4.  ferri
    5.  incavolato
    6.  dritto
    7.  bordello
    8.  sbirro
    9.  tappo
  10.  becco

B.   1.  b         9.  b
    2.  b     10.  a
    3.  b     11.  b
    4.  a     12.  a
    5.  a     13.  b
    6.  a     14.  a
    7.  a     15.  a
    8.  a     16.  a

C.   1.  bordello
    2.  dritto
    3.  tappo
    4.  fradicio
    5.  mani
    6.  scatole
    7.  sbirro
    8.  lavandino
    9.  ferri
  10.  incavolato
  11.  megagalattica
  12.  partito

D. **CROSSWORD PUZZLE**

## ANSWERS TO REVIEW EXAM 6-10

A.
| | | | |
|---|---|---|---|
| 1. a | 11. b | 21. a |
| 2. b | 12. a | 22. b |
| 3. b | 13. a | 23. b |
| 4. b | 14. b | 24. b |
| 5. b | 15. b | 25. b |
| 6. a | 16. a | 26. b |
| 7. b | 17. b | 27. b |
| 8. b | 18. a | 28. a |
| 9. a | 19. a | 29. b |
| 10. b | 20. a | 30. a |

B.
1. scatole
2. dritto
3. tappo
4. becco
5. matti
6. vita
7. carburo
8. tilt
9. birra
10. quattr'occhi
11. piove
12. tira

C.
1. E
2. B
3. D
4. I
5. A
6. F
7. C
8. G
9. J
10. H

D.
1. mani
2. lavandino
3. birra
4. scatole
5. giro
6. pasta
7. colpi
8. sbirro
9. pizza
10. sfondato
11. flippata
12. chetarsi

## APPENDIX

### -DICTATIONS-

### LEZIONE UNO

1. Faresti meglio a smettere di **fare forca** a scuola.

2. Se **scazzi** il prossimo test, i tuoi **vecchi** ti **fanno fuori**!

3. **Faccio sempre un buco nell'acqua**.

4. Vedi quella gran **bonazza**?

5. Hai sentito l'**ultima** su di lei?

6. Prima era la **protetta** del prof, ma ora non lo è più.

7. Il prof l'ha **presa in castagna** a copiare durante l'esame e ora lui la **sega**.

8. **Cavolo**! Sono sbalordito!

### LEZIONE DUE

1. Dove vai, così tutta **tirata**?

2. Che fai, esci con un **tipo** nuovo?

3. È un **secchionaccio della madonna!**

4. Non mi dire che **hai una bella cotta** per quello!

5. Eh, sì, **buona notte**!

6. Stasera sarà una **palla** indescrivibile!

7. Ma tu sei **di fuori**!

8. Che fortuna se mi **tirasse un bidone**!

## LEZIONE TRE

1. **Ammazza**! La tua macchina è davvero **spaziale**!

2. Che è successo alla tua vecchia **carcassa**?

3. Una vecchia **babbiona** tirava dritto giù per strada.

4. Mi ha **bocciato** con la sua macchina.

5. Ho **avuto un bel culo** che non mi ha **spappolato**!

6. Ho comprato questa incredibile **bomba** che **va come le sassate**.

7. Salta su, che ti do uno **strappo**.

8. Occhio però, a non farti **stoppare** dalla **pula** e a non finire **al fresco** per eccesso di velocità.

## LEZIONE QUATTRO

1. **Non ne posso più**!

2. Quello è davvero una **fogna**.

3. **Ha sempre una fame da lupo**.

4. **Sgrifa** tutto il giorno, poi **si abbiocca**.

5. C'era un **sacco** di cibo in frigo ieri.

6. Che **faccia tosta**!

7. Puzza **da morire** perchè **si tira** due pachetti di **paglie** al giorno.

8. Perchè non gli dici di **levarsi di torno**?

## LEZIONE CINQUE

1.  Vi state divertendo al mio **party**?

2.  È una gran **figata**!

3.  **Che palle**!

4.  **Ho fatto il pieno**! **Filiamocela**!

5.  Quello **ci prova** tutte le volte con me.

6.  Chi è quella **ciospa** con quei **trampoli** che gli sta vicino?

7.  Lei è diventata davvero una **balena**!

8.  Guarda come **si abbuffa come un maiale**!

## LEZIONE SEI

1.  Franco è un vero e proprio **armadio**.

2.  Giorgia è una **racchia** e una **pizza** tremenda!

3.  Tempo fa mi diceva che **non avevano un becco d'un quattrino**.

4.  Sono **ricchi sfondati**.

5.  Penso che lei sia una gran **ballista**.

6.  Forse è un po' **flippata** e magari va da uno **strizzacervelli**.

7.  Davvero sembra che sia un po' **balorda**.

8.  Puzzava **da fare schifo**.

## LEZIONE SETTE

1.  Devi essere davvero **fuori di testa**!

2.  Che **fregatura**!

3.  C'è qualcosa in questo negozio che ti **tira**?

4.  **Per carità**! Nulla!

5.  Ci ho **intoppato** Roberta Lariani.

6.  Mi sembra che si stia davvero **lasciando andare allo sbraco**!

7.  Sembra che stia **pappando** e bevendo un po'troppo.

8.  È davvero diventata una **scorfana**!

## LEZIONE OTTO

1.  Fra noi, **a quattr'occhi**, credo che sarà licenziato.

2.  Su questo **non ci piove**.

3.  Ho pensato che fosse una **pasta d'uomo.**

4.  I primi due giorni ha lavorato **a tutta birra**.

5.  Poi ha cominciato a **perdere colpi**.

6.  Ora sembra soltanto una **cariatide**.

7.  **Cincischia** e **non fa un fico** tutto il giorno.

8.  Oreste veniva a **sfacchinare** completamente **ciucco**!

## LEZIONE NOVE

1. **È una vita** che non ci vediamo!

2. **Non ho carburato** per una settimana.

3. All'inizio **mi sentivo soltanto un po'giù**.

4. Ho capito di essermi **buscato** l'influenza e allora sono **andato in tilt**.

5. Mi ero così scocciato a starmene **ibernato** in casa tutta la settimana.

6. Sono felice di vederti **in palla di nuovo**.

7. Quel film deve essere **la fine del mondo**.

8. Le commedie mi piacciono **da matti**!

## LEZIONE DIECI

1. Il cibo qui è **megagalattico**!

2. Ho pensato che fosse davvero **super bono**.

3. Ha **buttato giù tutto come un lavandino**.

4. Si è **incavolato** con il **buttafuori**.

5. Sono **venuti alle mani**.

6. Alla fine gli ha **allungato un dritto** nel **becco**.

7. Doveva essere o **ubriaco fradicio** o magari un po'**partito**.

8. Il tutto si è trasformato in un vero **bordello**.

# GLOSSARY

**a corto di qualcosa (essere)**
*exp.* to be short on something •
(lit.): to be at short of something.

example:
Mi piacerebbe andare al cinema
con te, ma questa settimana sono
**a corto di** soldi.

translation:
I'd like to go with you to the
movies, but **I'm short on** money
this week.

---

**a quattr'occhi** *exp.* just between
you and me • (lit.): at four eyes.

example:
Fra noi, **a quattr'occhi**, ho
saputo che Sergio vede un'altra
donna all'insaputa di sua moglie.

translation:
**Just between you and me**,
I heard that Sergio is seeing
another woman and his wife
doesn't suspect!

**NOTE:**
Although it may seem
redundant, *fra noi* (meaning
"between us") usually precedes
the expression *a quattr' occhi*, as
seen in the above example.

---

**a tutta birra** *adv.* with great
energy, at full throttle • (lit.): at
full beer (referring to the
"energetic" bubbling of the
beer's foam).

example:

Dobbiamo metterci a lavorare a **tutta birra** se vogliamo finire questo lavoro per le 5:00!

translation:

We have to work **full throttle** if we want to finish this job by 5:00!

**SYNONYM -1:**

**a palla** adv. • (lit.): like a ball (of energy).

**SYNONYM -2:**

**a tutto gas** adv. • (lit.): at full gasoline.

---

**abbioccarsi** v. to fall asleep, to doze off.

example:

Dopo cena Gianni ha bevuto due bicchieri di grappa e **si è abbioccato** subito sul divano.

translation:

After dinner Gianni had two glasses of grappa and **dozed off** right away on the couch.

---

**abbuffarsi come un maiale** exp. to stuff oneself like a pig.

example:

**Mi sono abbuffato come un maiale** alla festa, e ora mi sento male!

translation:

I **ate like a pig** at the party, and now I feel sick!

**accidente (un)** adv. nothing, "zip," "nada" • (lit.): accident, mishap.

example:

Sai cosa mi ha regalato Franco per il mio compleanno? **Un accidente**!

translation:

Do you know what Franco gave me for my birthday? **Zip**!

**SYNONYM -1:**

**nisba** adv. (Northern & Central Italy) • (lit.): from the German word *nichts*, meaning "nothing."

**SYNONYM -2:**

**ostia** f. • (lit.): host.

**SYNONYM -3:**

**un corno** m. • (lit.): a horn.

**SYNONYM -4:**

**un kaiser** m. • (lit.): a kaiser (from the German word, *Kaiser*, meaning "emperor").

**SYNONYM -5:**

**un tubo** m. (Central Italy) • (lit.): a tube.

**SYNONYM -6:**

**una madonna** f. • (lit.): a Madonna.

**SYNONYM -7:**

**una mazza** f. • (lit.): a sledgehammer.

---

**al fresco** adv. in jail, in the "cooler" • (lit.): in the cool [place].

example:
Il rapinatore passerà cinque anni **al fresco**.

translation:
The robber is going to spend five years in the **cooler**.

---

**alla grande** adj. beautifully, big-time • (lit.): to the big.

example:
– Sai se Mario ha passato l'esame?
– Sì, lo ha passato **alla grande**!

translation:
– Do you know if Mario passed his exam?
– Yes, he passed it **beautifully**!

---

**allocco/a** n. numbskull, idiot • (lit.): owl.

example:
Soltanto un **allocco** crederebbe a tutto quelo che dice Mario. Tutti sanno che lui è un bugiardo!

translation:
Only an **idiot** would believe anything that Mario says. Everyone knows he's a liar!

**VARIATION:**
**alloccone/a** n.

**SYNONYM -1:**
**babbeo/a** n.

**SYNONYM -2:**
**fesso/a** n. • (lit.): opening.

**SYNONYM -3:**
**oca** f. (only used in reference to a woman) • (lit.): goose.

**SYNONYM -4:**
**scimunito/a** n.

**SYNONYM -5:**
**sciocco/a** adj. • (lit.): bland.

---

**allungare un dritto** exp. to give someone a direct punch, to punch someone dead on • (lit.): to extend a straight.

example:
Quando ho detto a Matteo che non mi piaceva la sua macchina nuova, lui mi ha **allungato un dritto**!

translation:
When I told Matteo that I didn't like his new car, he **punched** me!

---

**Ammappa!** interj. Wow!

example:
**Ammappa**! È la casa più grande che io abbia mai visto!

translation:
**Wow**! That's the biggest house I've ever seen!

**SYNONYM -1:**
**Ammazza!** interj. (as introduced in Lesson Three, p. 51) • (lit.): from the verb *ammazzare*, meaning "to kill" – therefore the closest literal translation could be "Killer!"

**SYNONYM -2:**
**Capperi** interj. • (lit.): capers.

**SYNONYM -3:**
**Cavolo!** *interj.* (as introduced in Lesson One, p. 12) • (lit.): cabbage.

**SYNONYM -4:**
**Uah!** *interj.* a variation of the English "Wow!"

**SYNONYM -5:**
**Wow!** *interj.* (from English)

---

**Ammazza!** *interj.* Wow! • (lit.): from the verb *ammazzare,* meaning "to kill" – therefore the closest literal translation could be "Killer!"

example:
**Ammazza**! Hai visto quella stella cadente? Era così luminosa!

translation:
**Wow**! Did you see that shooting star? It was so bright!

**SYNONYM -1:**
**Ammappa!** *interj.*

**SYNONYM -2:**
**Capperi** *interj.* • (lit.): capers.

**SYNONYM -3:**
**Uah!** *interj.* a variation of the English "Wow!"

**SYNONYM -4:**
**Wow!** *interj.* (from English.)

---

**andare come le sassate** *exp.* to be extremely fast, to go as fast as a rocket • (lit.): to go like thrown stones or projectiles.

example:
Non riesco a credere come la gente guidi in questa città. **Vanno tutti come le sassate**!

translation:
I can't believe the way people drive in this city. **They all drive like bats out of hell**!

**NOTE:**
The masculine noun *sasso* means "stone." However, when the same stone is thrown, it is called *una sassata,* meaning "a thrown stone."

---

**andare in bianco** *exp.* not to get anywhere romantically with another person, not to "score" • (lit.): to go in white.

example:
– Come è andata la tua uscita con Alessandra?
– **In bianco**! Io non sono affatto il suo tipo!

translation:
– How was your date with Alessandra?
– **I didn't get anywhere**. I'm not her type at all.

---

**andare in tilt** *exp.* not to be oneself, to be out of it • (lit.): to feel on tilt (said of an arcade game that is nonfunctional).

example:
**Mi sento in tilt**. Spero di non prendermi l'influenza!

translation:
**I feel out of it**. I hope I'm not catching the flu!

**VARIATION:**

**fare tilt/sentirsi in tilt** *exp.* •
(lit.): to do tilt/to feel in tilt.

---

**armadio** *m.* tall and imposing man
• (lit.): closet.

example:
Filippa è molto piccola e magra,
mentre suo marito è un **armadio**.

translation:
Filippa is very small and thin, but
her husband is a **very tall and
imposing man**.

**ALSO -1:**

**lungagnone** *m.* (as introduced in
Lesson Two, p. 29) tall and lanky
man • (lit.): from *lungo,* meaning
"long."

**ALSO -2:**

**pennello** *m.* (Northern & Central
Italy) tall man • (lit.): paintbrush.

**VARIATION:**

**pennellone** *m.*

**ALSO -3:**

**pertica** *f.* • (lit.): pole.

**ALSO -4:**

**perticone** *m.* from *pertica,*
meaning "pole."

**ALSO -5:**

**stanga** *f.* • (lit.): bar.

---

**arrivare al capolinea** *exp.* to
be at death's door • (lit.): to arrive
at the terminal.

example:
– Non ti vedo da una settimana!
Dove sei stato?
– Ero a casa con l'influenza!
Pensavo di essere **arrivato
al capolinea**!

translation:
– I haven't seen you for a
week! Where have you been?
– I was sick at home with the flu.
I thought I was **at death's
door**!

**SYNONYM:**

**essere alla frutta** *exp.* • (lit.):
to be at the fruit.

**babbiona** *f.* crotchety old
woman, old geezer.

example:
La mia prima maestra di
pianoforte era una [vecchia]
**babbiona** che mi faceva
suonare musica che odiavo. Ora
ho una maestra giovane che mi
fa suonare quello che voglio!

translation:
The first piano teacher I ever
had was this [old] **geezer** who
made me play music I hated.
Now I have a young teacher
who lets me play whatever
I want!

**NOTE:**
**babbione** *m.* crotchety old man, old fart.

**SYNONYM:**
**bavoso/a** *n.* • (lit.): slobbering (from the verb *sbavare,* meaning "to slobber").

---

**balena** *f.* fat woman, "blimp" • (lit.): whale.

example:
Che è successo a Roberta? Prima era magrissima e ora è una **balena**!

translation:
What happened to Roberta? She used to be so thin and now she's a **blimp**!

**VARIATION:**
**balenottera** *f.*

---

**balenottera** *f.* fatso • (lit.): a variation of *balena (as introduced in Lesson Five, p. 78),* meaning "whale."

example:
Ora capisco perchè Carlotta è così **balenottera**. Non fa che mangiare!

translation:
Now I understand why Carlotta is such a **fatso**. She never stops eating!

---

**ballista** *f.* liar • (lit.): from *balle,* meaning "lies," or literally, "bales."

example:
Non puoi credere a niente di quello che Roberto ti dice. Lui è un **ballista**!

translation:
You can't believe anything Roberto says to you. He's a **liar**!

**NOTE:**
**una balla** *f.* a cock-and-bull story.

---

**balordo/a** *n.* crackpot, nut, blockhead.

example:
Sono proprio **balordo**! Oggi ho chiuso la macchina con le chiavi dentro, due volte!

translation:
I'm such a **blockhead**. I locked my keys in the car for the second time this week!

**SYNONYM:**
**baccalà** *m.* • (lit.): dried fish.

---

**barche** *f.pl.* old, worn-out shoes • (lit.): boats.

example:
Quando butterai via quelle **barche** e ti comprerai un paio di scarpe nuove?

translation:
When are you going to throw away those **old, worn-out shoes** and get some new ones?

**barilotto** *m.* (applied usually only to a man) short, fat man • (lit.): small keg.

example:
Matteo è un **barilotto**, mentre sua moglie è alta e snella.

translation:
Filippo is a **short, fat guy**, but his wife is tall and slender.

**SYNONYM:**
**buzzino** *m.* (as seen in Lesson Five) short, fat man with a potbelly • (lit.): from *buzza*, meaning "belly."

---

**bavoso/a** *n.* old geezer, old fart • (lit.): drooler (from the verb *sbavare*, meaning "to drool").

example:
Quel vecchio **bavoso** in fondo alla strada era un atleta olimpionico. Da non crederci!

translation:
That **old geezer** down the street used to be an Olympic athlete. It's hard to believe!

**SYNONYM:**
**babbione/a** *n.*

---

**beccare** *v.* to call on someone in class (said of a teacher) • (lit.): to peck.

example:
L'insegnante mi ha **beccato** sei volte oggi e non ho risposto bene nemmeno una volta!

translation:
The teacher **called on me** six times today and I never got the right answer once!

**SYNONYM:**
**blindare** *v.* • (lit.): to armor (with metal plates).

**ALSO:**
**beccare** *v.* to catch or pick up (an illness, etc.).

---

**becco d'un quattrino (non avere un)** *exp.* not to have a red cent • (lit.): not to have a beak of a penny.

example:
Quando i miei nonni sono arrivati in questo paese, non avevano il **becco d'un quattrino**. Ora invece sono proprietari di un bel negozio.

translation:
When my grandparents came to this country, they **didn't have a red cent**. Now they own a successful business.

**VARIATION:**
**restare senza il becco d'un quattrino** *exp.* to remain without a beak of a penny.

**SYNONYM:**
**spennato/a** *adj.* (as introduced in Lesson Three, p. 47) broke • (lit.): plucked.

**NOTE:**
A *quattrino* was an old coin made of copper in the mid-thirteenth century that had little value, like a penny.

**becco** *m.* mouth • (lit.): beak.

example:

Chiudi il **becco**! Non dici altro che bugie!

translation:

Shut your **mouth**! All you ever do is lie!

---

**bocciare** *v.* to crash into someone • (lit.): to knock away the opponent's wooden ball in the game of bocce.

example:

La mia nuova macchina è rovinata. Un tipo, passando col rosso, me l'ha **bocciata**!

translation:

My new car is ruined. Some guy went through a red light and **bashed into** it!

**NOTE:**
As seen in Lesson One, the verb *bocciare* can also be used to mean "to flunk."

**SYNONYM -1:**
**arrotare** *v.* • (lit.): to sharpen.

**SYNONYM -2:**
**stendere** *v.* to hit a pedestrian with a vehicle • (lit.): to spread.

---

**bomba** *f.* a blast (of fun) • (lit.): a bomb.

example:

Mi sono divertito moltissimo al Luna Park. Che **bomba**!

translation:

I had a great time at the amusement park. What a **blast**!

**SYNONYM:**
**cannonata** *f.* • (lit.): cannon shot.

**ALSO:**
**una bomba** *f.* a tall tale or lie.

**NOTE:**
**tirare una bomba** *exp.* to tell a lie • (lit.): to tell a lie.

---

**bomba** *f.* said of any fantastic possession • (lit.): a bomb.

example:

Che **bomba** di macchina hai! Ne ho sempre desiderata una uguale!

translation:

What a **great car** you have! I've always wanted one just like it!

**NOTE:**
As seen in Lesson Two, the noun *bomba* can also be used to mean "a blast (of fun)."

---

**bonazza** *f.* a girl who is extremely pretty to the point of being overdone, "bombshell" (which comes from the adjective *buono/bono [buona/bona],* meaning "good") • (lit.): a really good thing.

example:

L'ex ragazza di Antonio era davvero brutta, ma quella nuova è una gran **bonazza**!

translation:

Antonio's old girlfriend was really ugly, but his new one is a real **bombshell**!

**NOTE:**

The suffix -*azza* is commonly attached to certain nouns to add a sarcastic connotation.

---

**bordello** *m.* uproar, hubbub • (lit.): brothel.

example:

Che **bordello** c'è là fuori? Sembra che qualcuno se le stia dando!

translation:

What's the **uproar** outside? It sounds like someone is having a fight!

**SYNONYM -1:**

**baccano** *m.* • (lit.): from Bacchus (the Greek god of parties).

**SYNONYM -2:**

**caciara** *f.*

**SYNONYM -3:**

**cagnara** *f.*

**SYNONYM -4:**

**casino** *m.* • (lit.): brothel.

**SYNONYM -5:**

**chiasso** *m.*

**SYNONYM -6:**

**fracasso** *m.*

**SYNONYM -7:**

**gazzarra** *f.*

---

**bottega aperta (avere la)**

*exp.* to have one's zipper open unintentionally • (lit.): to have one's shop open.

example:

L'insegnante **ha la bottega aperta**! Mi domando se qualcuno in classe avrà il coraggio di dirglielo!

translation:

The teacher's **fly is open**! I wonder if anyone in the class will have the nerve to tell him!

---

**Buona notte!** *interj.* No way! You've got to be kidding! Oh, brother! • (lit.): Good night!

example:

Simona esce con Marco? **Buona notte**! Lui ha il doppio degli anni di lei!

translation:

Simona is dating Marco? **Oh, brother**! He's twice as old as she is!

**SYNONYM:**

**Non esiste!** *interj.* • (lit.): It doesn't exist!

---

**burino** *m.* a crude, ill-bred individual.

example:

Piero è andato a una cena molto elegante con una giacca bianca e un mazzetto di banconote da cento dollari che gli uscivano dal taschino. Che **burino**!

translation:
Piero went to a very formal gala dinner wearing a white jacket with a bunch of $100 bills sticking out of his pocket. What a **tacky person**.

---

**buscarsi** *v.* to catch something unpleasant • (lit.): to find oneself.

example:
Mi farebbe piacere venire con te al cinema, ma ieri **mi sono buscato** un raffreddore e farei meglio a starmene a casa.

translation:
I'd like to go with you to the movies but yesterday I **caught** a cold and should probably just stay home.

---

**buttafuori** *m.* bouncer (in a bar, hotel, etc.) • (lit.): from *buttare*, meaning "to throw" and *fuori*, meaning "out."

example:
Ieri sera Francesco era così ubriaco e rumoroso che il **buttafuori** lo ha cacciato!

translation:
Last night, Francesco got so drunk and loud that the **bouncer** threw him out!

ANTONYM: **buttadentro** *m.* the bouncer who greets people at the door and allows only those who are authorized to enter • (lit.): the "throw inside."

**buttare giù tutto come un lavandino** *exp.* to eat like a pig • (lit.): to thrown down everything as if one were a sink.

example:
Maria **butta giù tutto come un lavandino**, ma ciò nonostante è sempre magra!

translation:
Maria **eats like she has a hollow leg**, but she's still so thin!

---

**buzzino** *m.* short, fat man with a potbelly • (lit.): from *buzza*, meaning "belly."

example:
Se continui a bere birra, diventerai un **buzzino**!

translation:
If you keep drinking beer all the time, you're going to turn into a **short, fat guy with a pot-belly**!

---

# C

**capoccia** *m.* boss, foreman, head of the house • (lit.): from *capo*, meaning "head, chief, leader, etc."

example:

Luigi mi ha fatto chiamare dal **capoccia** per essere arrivato tardi a lavoro.

translation:

Luigi reported me to the **boss** for arriving late to work.

---

**carburare** *v.* to feel well • (lit.): to carburate.

example:

**Non carburo**. Penso che dovrei andare a casa e mettermi a letto.

translation:

**I don't feel well**. I think I'd better go home and go to bed.

---

**carcassa** *f.* ramshackle car • (lit.): carcass.

example:

Mi piace la tua macchina nuova! Che fine ha fatto la tua vecchia **carcassa**?

translation:

I love your new car! What did you do with your old **carcass**?

**SYNONYM -1:**

**bagnarola** *f.* (Northern & Central Italy) • (lit.): from the popular French slang term for car: *bagnole*.

**SYNONYM -2:**

**carretta** *f.* • (lit.): two-wheeled cart, wheelbarrow.

**SYNONYM -3:**

**catorcio** *m.* • (lit.): old thing in bad shape.

**cariatide** *f.* said of a person who just stands there and doesn't offer to help, deadweight • (lit.): caryatid (a supporting column carved in the shape of a person).

example:

Guido ed io abbiamo fatto tutto il lavoro, mentre Aldo stava lì a guardare! Lui non è altro che una **cariatide**!

translation:

Guido and I did all the work while Aldo just stood there watching! He's nothing but **deadweight**!

---

**casino (fare)** *exp.* to make a lot of noise • (lit.): to make a brothel.

example:

I miei vicini hanno avuto una festa ieri sera e hanno **fatto un gran casino**. Non sono riuscito a dormire un minuto!

translation:

The neighbors had a big party and made **a lot of noise**. I couldn't sleep a minute!

**NOTE:**

You'll notice in the dialogue that the indefinite article *"un"* was used before *casino*. Whenever *casino* is modified by an adjective, in this case *incredibile*, *"un"* must precede *casino*.

---

**casino di roba** *exp.* a lot of stuff • (lit.): a brothel of stuff.

example:

Ho portato indietro con me un **casino di roba** dalle vacanze. Sono riuscito a mala pena a fare entrare tutto in valigia!

translation:

I brought a **ton of stuff** back with me from my vacation. I could hardly fit it all in my suitcase!

**NOTE:**

The noun **roba** can be used in reference to anything unspecific just as "stuff" is used in English.

---

**Cavolo!** *interj.* Wow! • (lit.): cabbage.

example:

**Cavolo**! Che ragazza stupenda!

translation:

**Wow**! What an awesome girl!

**SYNONYM:**

**Capperi!** *interj.* • (lit.): capers.

---

**cenci** *m.pl.* ugly clothing • (lit.): piece of cloth (from the masculine noun *cencio*, meaning "cloth").

example:

Hai visto i **cenci** che Carolina aveva addosso alla festa? Era ridicola!

translation:

Did you see the **ugly clothes** Carolina was wearing to the party? She looked ridiculous!

**SYNONYM:**

**non essere nei propri cenci** *exp.* to feel out of it, out of sorts • (lit.): not to be in one's clothes.

---

**Che palle!** *inter.* What a drag! • (lit.): What balls!

example:

Le feste di Annamaria sono sempre le peggiori! **Che palle**! Andiamocene!

translation:

Annamaria always has the worst parties. **What a drag**! Let's get out of here!

**VARIATION:**

**Che palloso/a!** *interj.*

**SYNONYM -1:**

**Che coma!** *interj.* • (lit.): What a coma!

**SYNONYM -2:**

**Che depressione!** *interj.* • (lit.): What a depression!

**SYNONYM -3:**

**Che mattone!** *interj.* • (lit.): What a brick!

**SYNONYM -4:**

**Che peso/a!** *interj.* (Northern & Central Italy) • (lit.): What heaviness.

**SYNONYM -4:**

**Che pizza!** *interj.* • (lit.): What a pizza!

**SYNONYM -5:**

**Che rottura!** *interj.* • (lit.): What a breaking! (from the verb *rompere*, meaning "to break").

**chetarsi** *v.* to shut up • (lit.): to grow calm, to abate.

example:

In aereo, ero seduto accanto a una signora che non **si è chetata** per tutto il volo!

translation:

On the airplane, I sat next to a woman who wouldn't **shut up** the entire flight!

---

**chiacchierone/a** *n.* blabbermouth • (lit.): from the verb *chiacchierare*, meaning "to chatter."

example:

C'è Carolina! Se mi vede quella non finisce più di parlare. Lei è così **chiacchierona**!

translation:

There's Carolina! If she sees me, she'll talk forever. She's such a **blabbermouth**!

**VARIATION:**

**chiacchierino/a** *n.*

**SYNONYM:**

**mitragliatrice** *f.* said of someone who speaks very quickly • (lit.): machine gun.

**ALSO -1:**

**chiacchiera** *f.* chatter, gossip, chit-chat.

**VARIATION:**

**chiacchierata** *f.*

**ALSO -2:**

**Chiacchiere!** *interj.* Nonsense!

**cima** *f.* a genius, a "brain" • (lit.): top.

example:

Anna ha finito tutti i problemi in meno di dieci minuti! Lei è davvero una **cima**!

translation:

Anna finished all the problems in less than ten minutes! She is really a **brain**!

---

**cincischiare** *v.* to waste time doing nothing productive • (lit.): to chop; to dawdle.

example:

Invece di darsi da fare per trovare un lavoro, Simona se ne è andata in giro a **cincischiare**.

translation:

Instead of looking for a job, Simona just **hung out and did nothing**.

**SYNONYM:**

**gingillarsi** *v.* • (lit.): to fiddle, to loaf.

---

**ciospo/a** *n.* ugly person, "troll."

example:

Hai visto Paola? È diventata una **ciospa**!

translation:

Did you see Paola? She has turned into an **ugly troll**!

**SYNONYM -1:**

**racchio/a** *adj.*

**SYNONYM -2:**

**scorfano/a** *n.* • (lit.): scorpion fish.

---

**ciucco/a** *adj.* drunk, plastered.

example:
Sergio è venuto a casa mia completamente **ciucco**!

translation:
Sergio came to my house totally **plastered**!

**SYNONYM -1:**

**avvinazzato/a** *adj.* (from *vino*, meaning "wine").

**SYNONYM -2:**

**briaco/a** *adj.* (a Tuscan variation of *ubriaco*, meaning "inebriated").

**VARIATION:**

**briaco fradicio / briaca fradicia** *exp.* stinking drunk, totally plastered • (lit.): rotten drunk.

**SYNONYM -3:**

**brillo/a** *adj.* • (lit.): shiny.

**SYNONYM -4:**

**sbronzo/a** *adj.*

**ALSO:**

**prendere una ciucca** *exp.* to get very drunk • *Se bevo più di un bicchiere di vino, mi prendo una ciucca*; If I drink more than one glass of wine, I get plastered.

**cotta per qualcuno (avere una)** *exp.* to have a crush on someone • (lit.): to have a baking for someone (from the feminine noun *cottura*, meaning "cooking" or "baking").

example:
Credo che Giovanni **abbia una cotta per me**, perchè mi segue ovunque!

translation:
I think Giovanni **has a crush on me**, because he follows me everywhere!

**VARIATION:**

**prendere una cotta per qualcuno** *exp.* • (lit.): to take a baking for someone.

**NOTE:**

**Sono cotto per lei** ("I am baked for her") [or] **Ho una cotta per lei** ("I have a baking for her") – Note that cotta is an adjective in the first example (which is why it changed to *cotto*) and is a noun in the second example (which is why it remains *cotta* even if said by a man).

**SYNONYM -1:**

**avere una fissa per qualcuno** *exp.* • (lit.): to have an obsession for someone.

**NOTE:**

The feminine adjective *fissa* is an abbreviation of *fissazione*, meaning "obsession."

**SYNONYM -2:**

**prendere una scuffia per qualcuno** *exp.* • (lit.): to take a capsizing for someone.

---

**culo (avere un gran)** *exp.* to be very lucky • (lit.): to have a big ass.

example:
Alberto si è rotto il collo, ma ha anche **avuto un gran culo**, perchè si tratta soltanto di una lieve frattura.

translation:
Alberto broke his neck but was **very lucky**. It was only a minor fracture.

**NOTE -1:**

Although this expression uses the masculine noun *culo*, literally meaning "ass," its connotation is not as strong as in English. It is important to remember that by European standards, Americans are considered somewhat prudish and many terms that would be considered highly offensive in the United States, are quite acceptable in other countries such as Italy.

**NOTE -2:**

You may have noticed that in the dialogue, the adjective *bel* was used in the expression: "*Ho avuto un bel culo…*" This is an extremely popular usage of *bel/bella*, used to mean: **1.** a real…; • **2.** smack dab. For example: **1.** *Gino è un bell'idiota!*; Gino is a real idiot! • **2.** *nel bel mezzo della notte;* smack dab in the middle of the night.

**VARIATION:**

**avere un culo bestiale** *exp.* to be extremely lucky • (lit.): to have beastly luck (ass).

**SYNONYM:**

**avere fondello** *exp.* (Central Italy) • (lit.): to have bottom.

---

**culo a qualcuno (stare sul)** *exp.* to bug someone big-time • (lit.): to be on someone's ass.

example:
Il fratellino di Franco **mi sta davvero sul culo**. Mi segue dappertutto!

translation:
Franco's little brother really **bugs me**. He follows me everywhere!

**NOTE:**

As mentioned earlier, although this expression uses the masculine noun *culo*, literally meaning "ass," its connotation is not as strong as in English. It's important to remember that by European standards, Americans are considered somewhat prudish and many terms that would be considered highly offensive in the United States, are quite acceptable in other countries such as Italy.

**da fare schifo** *exp.* said of something disgusting • (lit.): from making disgust.

example:
Questo liquore è forte **da fare schifo**!

translation:
This liquor is **disgustingly strong**!

**NOTE:**
The expression **da fare schifo** always follows an adjective as opposed to **fare schifo**, also meaning "to be disgusting," which stands alone. For example:

example:
Ora capisco perchè questo albergo è così economico. **Fa schifo**!

translation:
Now I understand why this hotel is so inexpensive. **It's disgusting**!

**ALSO:**
**prendere in schifo** *exp.* to take an immediate dislike to someone or something.

---

**da morire** *adj.* (used to modify a noun or verb) big-time • (lit.): from dying.

example:
Questo caffè è buono **da morire**!

translation:
This coffee is **to die for**!

**dare/fare una ripassata a qualcuno** *exp.* to reprimand someone, to rake someone over the coals, to call someone on the carpet • (lit.): to give/do someone a revision.

example:
Laura **ha dato una ripassata a suo figlio** perchè lui le aveva detto una bugia.

translation:
Laura **raked her son over the coals** for lying to her.

**SYNONYM -1:**
**dare/fare una cazziata a qualcuno** *exp.*

**SYNONYM -2:**
**dare/fare una cazziatone a qualcuno** *exp.*

**SYNONYM -3:**
**dare/fare una lavata di capo a qualcuno** *exp.* to give a raking over the coals to someone • (lit.): to give/do someone a washing of the head.

**SYNONYM -4:**
**dare/fare una ramanzina a qualcuno** *exp.* • (lit.): to give/do someone a telling off.

---

**della madonna** *exp.* big-time, in a major way • (lit.): of the Madonna.

example:
Francesca mi ha detto di avere sangue blu. Lei è una bugiarda **della madonna**.

translation:
Francesca told me that she comes from royalty. She's **such a big-time** liar.

**NOTE:**
In the example above, *sangue blu* (literally translated as "blue blood") was used to mean "royalty" just as it is in English.

**SYNONYM -1:**
**alla grande** *exp.* • (lit.): to the big.

**SYNONYM -2:**
**il massimo / la massima** *exp.* • (lit.): the maximum • *Questa pizza è il massimo!;* This pizza is the best!

---

**di fuori (essere)** *exp.* to be crazy • (lit.): to be out (of one's mind).

example:
Hai guidato senza occhiali? Sei **fuori di testa**? Avresti potuto fare un incidente!

translation:
You drove me without your glasses? Are you **out of your mind**? You could have gotten into an accident!

**SYNONYM -1:**
**flippato/a** *adj.* • (lit.): flipped.

**SYNONYM -2:**
**girare** *v.* (Central Italy) • (lit.): to turn • *Ma ti gira il cervello?;* Are you nuts? (lit.): Is your brain turning?).

**faccia tosta** *exp.* nerve, brazenness • (lit.): toasted face.

example:
Paolo mi ha dapprima insultato ed offeso durante l'intera conversazione, poi mi ha invitato alla sua festa. Che **faccia tosta** che ha!

translation:
First Paolo insulted me and swore at me during the whole conversation, then he invited me to his party! What **nerve**!

---

**fame da lupo (avere una)** *exp.* to be extremely hungry • (lit.): to have a hunger of a wolf.

example:
A che ora ceniamo? **Ho una fame da lupo**!

translation:
What time are we eating dinner? **I'm starving**!

---

**fare forca** *exp.* to cut class • (lit.): to do the gallows.

example:
Non ho visto Alberto a scuola oggi. Mi domando se abbia **fatto forca**.

translation:
I haven't seen Alberto in school today. I wonder if he **cut class**.

**SYNONYM -1:**
**bigiare** *v.* (Northern Italy)

**SYNONYM -2:**
**bucare** *v.* (Northern & Central Italy) • (lit.): to make a hole (to escape through).

**SYNONYM -3:**
**fare sega** *exp.* (Rome & Central Italy) • (lit.): to do the saw (i.e. to cut out).

**fare i gattini** *exp.* to vomit, to barf • (lit.): to make the kittens.

example:
Ho dei disturbi di stomaco. Spero di non **fare i gattini** proprio qui al cinema!

translation:
My stomach is upset. I hope I don't **barf** right here in the movie theater!

**fare fuori** *exp.* to kill, to waste (someone), to take out someone (as in "to kill") • (lit.): to make outside.

example:
Federico ha paura che il ladro lo **faccia fuori**, per il fatto di essere stato testimone oculare del furto.

translation:
Federico is scared that the thief is going **to kill him** for witnessing the crime.

**SYNONYM -1:**
**far la festa a qualcuno** *exp.* • (lit.): to give someone a (good-bye) party.

**SYNONYM -2:**
**fare secco qualcuno** *exp.* • (lit.): to make someone dry.

**SYNONYM -3:**
**fare una frittata** *exp.* • (lit.): to make an omelette out of someone.

**SYNONYM -4:**
**stendere qualcuno** *exp.* • (lit.): to lay someone down.

**fare il pieno** *exp.* to have had all one can tolerate • (lit.): to make the full (commonly used in reference to filling a car's gas tank).

example:
**Ho fatto il pieno**! Tutte le volte che vado da Anna, lei mi vuol far sapere quanti soldi ha. È davvero offensivo!

translation:
**I've had it**! Everytime I go to Ana's house, she brags about how much money she has. It's really offensive!

**fare il ruffiano/la ruffiana** *exp.* to butter someone up • (lit.): to do like a pimp/madame.

example:
Marco **fa il ruffiano** con il capo perchè ha intenzione di chiedergli un aumento.

translation:
Marco is **buttering up** the boss because he's going to ask him for a raise.

translation:
How did the boss find out you came in late today? Did someone **snitch**?

---

**fare un buco nell'acqua** *exp.* to be totally unsuccessful, to botch up something • (lit.): to make a hole in the water.

example:
Ogni volta che provo ad aggiustare la mia macchina, **faccio un buco nell'acqua**. La prossima volta vado da un meccanico!

translation:
Every time I try to fix my car, **I botch it up**. Next time, I'm going to a mechanic!

**ALSO:**
**tappare un buco** *exp.* to pay a debt • (lit.): to fill a hole.

---

**fare una soffiata** *exp.* to report someone, to rat on someone, "to blow the whistle on someone" • (lit.): to do the blow (from the verb *soffiare*, meaning "to blow").

**SYNONYM -1:**
**fare una spifferata** *exp.* • (lit.): to do a gust.

example:
Come ha fatto a sapere il capo che tu sei arrivato a lavoro tardi oggi? Qualcuno ha **fatto una soffiata**?

---

**farsi il culo** *exp.* to work extremely hard, to bust one's butt • (lit.): to do one's ass.

example:
**Mi sono fatto il culo** per tre mesi, per cercare di finire il progetto. Ho perfino lavorato durante i fine settimana, ma il capo non mi ha nemmeno ringraziato!

translation:
I **busted my butt** for three months in order to get this project done. I even worked on weekends and the boss didn't even thank me!

**NOTE:**
Remember, although this expression uses the masculine noun *culo* literally meaning "ass," its connotation is <u>not</u> as strong as in English. It is important to remember that by European standards, Americans are considered somewhat prudish and many terms that would be considered highly offensive in the United States, are quite acceptable in other countries such as Italy.

**SYNONYM:**
**darci dentro** *exp.* to work or study very hard • (lit.): to give oneself inside.

**farsi una bevutina** *exp.* to have a drink • (lit.): to make oneself a little drink (from *bevuta*, meaning "a drink").

example:
Vogliamo andare a **farci una bevutina** prima di andare al cine?

translation:
Would you like to go **get a drink** before we go to the movie?

---

**fasullo** • **1.** *adj.* phony • **2.** *m.* a fake, a faker.

example:
Non mi fido di Massimo, perchè penso che sia un po' **fasullo**!

translation:
I don't trust Massimo. I think he's a little **phony**.

---

**ferri** *m.pl.* handcuffs • (lit.): irons.

example:
Ho appena visto la polizia portare Marcello con i **ferri**! Chissà cosa ha fatto!

translation:
I just saw Marcello get taken away in **handcuffs** by the cops! I wonder what he did!

---

**fesso/a** *n.* jerk, dimwit, dolt, fool • (lit.): from the verb *fendere*, meaning "to split" – therefore, a rough translation could be "someone who is split in the head" or "someone who has half a brain."

example:
Marcello è un esperto di automobili. Non riesco veramente a credere che sia stato così **fesso** a comprare quella carcassa per 5.000 dollari!

translation:
Marcello is a car expert. I am really surprised that he was so **stupid** to buy a wreck for $5,000!

**NOTE:**
In large numbers, the comma is used in English whereas in Italian, the period is used. For example: *(English)* 5,000 = *(Italian)* 5.000.

---

**figata** *f.* an extremely positive situation or thing, a very "cool" thing.

example:
– Ti è piaciuta la festa di Salvatore?
– Sì! È stata una vera **figata**!

translation:
– Did you like Salvatore's party?
– Yes! It was a **blast**!

**SYNONYM -1:**
**bomba** *f.* • (lit.): bomb.

**SYNONYM -2:**
**cannonata** *f.* • (lit.): cannon shot.

---

**figo** *m.* handsome guy, hunk.

example:
Hai visto il nuovo ragazzo di Giovanna? È così **figo**!

translation:
Did you see Giovanna's new boyfriend? He's such a **hunk**!

**VARIATION:**
**figone** m.

---

**filarsela** v. to leave quickly, to scram• (lit.): to spin oneself to it.

example:
Suona l'allarme! **Filiamocela** prima che la polizia ci veda!

translation:
The alarm went off! **Let's scram** before the cops see us!

**SYNONYM -1:**
**alzare le fette** exp. • (lit.): to lift one's feet.

**SYNONYM -2:**
**battersela** v. • (lit.): to beat oneself it.

**SYNONYM -3:**
**darsela** v. • (lit.): to give oneself to it.

**ALSO:**
**darsela a gambe** exp. to run away quickly • to give it to oneself to the legs.

**SYNONYM -4:**
**schizzare** v. • (lit.): to squirt.

---

**fine del mondo (la)** exp.
fantastic, awesome, out of this world • (lit.): the end of the world.

example:
Paolo mi ha portato a un ottimo ristorante per il mio compleanno. Il cibo era **la fine del mondo**!

translation:
Paolo took me to a great restaurant for my birthday. The food was **out of this world**!

---

**flippato/a** adj. (from English) crazy, flipped out • (lit.): flipped (from the verb flipparsi, meaning "to flip out").

example:
Come mai quell'uomo sta parlando ad un lampione? Deve essere **flippato**!

translation:
Why is that man talking to that lamppost? He must be **flipped out**!

**NOTE:**
The adjective flippato/a can also be used in slang to mean "flipped out on drugs."

**SYNONYM:**
**di fuori (essere)** exp. (as introduced in Lesson Two, p. 28) to be crazy • (lit.): to be out (of one's mind).

---

**fogna (essere una)** f. to be a bottomless pit, said of someone who will swallow anything literally and metaphorically • (lit.): to be a sewer.

example:
Davide ha mangiato tutto quello che c'era nel frigo e ha ancora fame. È proprio una **fogna**!

translation:
David ate everything in the refrigerator and he's still hungry! What a **bottomless pit**!

**SYNONYM:**

**cloaca** f. • (lit.): sewer, drain, cesspool.

---

**frana** f. a failure (when referring to a person) • (lit.): landslide.

example:
Questa è la terza volta che Franco viene licenziato questo mese. È davvero una **frana**.

translation:
This is the third time this month that Franco got fired from a job. He's such a **loser**.

---

**fregatura** f. thievery, rip-off.

example:
Hai visto il prezzo su quella giacca? Che **fregatura**!

translation:
Did you see the price for that jacket? What a **rip-off**!

---

**fuori di testa (essere)** exp. to be crazy • (lit.): to be out of one's head.

example:
Esci con Martina? Ma sei **fuori di testa**? Lei ha già un ragazzo, per giunta il più grosso della scuola!

translation:
You're going out with Martina? Are you **out of your mind**? She already has a boyfriend who is the biggest guy in school!

**SYNONYM -1:**

**di fuori (essere)** exp. (as introduced in Lesson Two, p. 28) • (lit.): to be out (of one's mind).

**SYNONYM -2:**

**flippato/a** adj. • (lit.): flipped.

**SYNONYM -3:**

**girare** v. (Central Italy) • (lit.): to turn • *Ma ti gira il cervello?*; Are you nuts? (lit.): Is your brain turning?

**gabbia** f. • **1.** jail, "slammer" • **2.** loony bin • (lit.): cage.

example:
Il fratelo di Stefania starà in **gabbia** per un anno per aver guidato in stato di ebbrezza!

translation:
Stefania's brother is going to be in the **slammer** for a year for drunk driving!

**SYNONYM -1:**
**al fresco** *m.* • (lit.): in the cool (as in, "to cool one's heels").

**SYNONYM -2:**
**essere dentro** *exp.* • (lit.): to be inside.

**ibernarsi** *v.* to stay cooped up in one place • (lit.): to hibernate.

example:
Perchè non vieni a ballare con noi stasera? Non sei stanco di startene **ibernato** in casa tutto il giorno?

translation:
Why don't you join us tonight and go dancing? Aren't you tired of being **cooped up** in your house all day?

---

**in gamba (essere)** *exp.* to be on the ball • (lit.): to be in leg.

example:
Alessio è un bravissimo medico. Lui riesce a fornire diagnosi più accurate di quelle della maggior parte degli altri medici. È davvero **in gamba**!

translation:
Alessio is a great doctor. He can diagnose a patient more accurately than most doctors. He's really **on the ball**!

---

**impiombare** *v.* to shoot someone dead • (lit.): to fill with lead (from the verb *piombare*, meaning "to cover with lead").

example:
Sono così stufo dei western dove alla fine tutti finiscono **impiombati**.

translation:
I'm so tired of westerns where everyone ends up getting **shot dead**.

---

**incavolarsi** *v.* to fly off the handle, to get ticked off • (lit.): to throw oneself in the cabbage (from *cavolo*, meaning "cabbage").

example:
**Mi sono incavolato** con mio fratello perchè ha preso la mia macchina senza chiedermela.

translation:
I **flew off the handle** with my brother because he borrowed my car without asking me.

**SYNONYM:**
**imbestialirsi** *v.* to become a *bestia*, meaning "beast."

**intoppare qualcuno** *v.* to see someone unexpectedly, to bump into someone • (lit.): to bump someone.

example:
Non indovinerai mai chi ho **intoppato** oggi – il mio primo ragazzo! Non lo vedevo da vent'anni!

translation:
You'll never guess who I **bumped into** today – my first boyfriend! I haven't seen him in twenty years!

**kaput** *adj.* (from German) broken, "kaput."

example:
Il mio computer è **kaput**. Dovrò comprarmene uno nuovo quando avrò un po' di soldi.

translation:
My computer is **kaput**. I'm going to have to buy a new one as soon as I have the money.

**lanciarsi** *v.* to get the courage to do something, to get up one's nerve • (lit.): to hurl oneself.

example:
Quella ragazza mi piace molto. Devo **lanciarmi** perchè voglio invitarla ad uscire con me.

translation:
I really like that girl. I need to **get up my nerve** because I want to invite her to go out with me.

**ALSO:**
**lanciare un'idea** *exp.* to make a suggestion • (lit.): to throw an idea.

---

**lasciarsi andare allo sbraco** *exp.* to let oneself go • (lit.): to let oneself go sloppy.

example:
Franesca si è **lasciata andare allo sbraco**! Era così carina una volta!

translation:
Francesca has **let herself go**! She used to be so pretty!

---

**levarsi di torno** *exp.* to leave a place, to "beat it" • (lit.): to get oneself up from around here.

example:
**Levati di torno**! Non dovresti essere qui!

translation:
**Get out of here**! You're not supposed to be here!

**SYNONYM -1:**
**alzare i tacchi** *exp.* to get moving • (lit.): to lift one's heels • *Alza i tacchi!*; Get lost!

**SYNONYM -2:**
**Aria!** *interj.* Get lost! • (lit.): air.

**SYNONYM -3:**
**circolare** *v.* • (lit.): to circulate • (lit.): *Circola!*; Get lost!

**SYNONYM -4:**
**scarpinare** *v.* • (lit.): to move one's shoes • *Scarpina!*; Get lost!

**SYNONYM -5:**
**smammare** *v.* (from Naples) • *Smamma!*; Get lost!

---

**lungagnone** *m.* a tall and lanky person (from the adjective *lungo*, meaning "long," "tall," etc.), "beanpole."

example:
Davide, da bambino era basso e grassottello. Ora invece è un **lungagnone**!

translation:
When David was a little boy, he was short and overweight. Now he's a **beanpole**!

**SYNONYM -1:**
**pertica** *f.* • (lit.): pole.

**SYNONYM -2:**
**perticone** *m.* from *pertica*, meaning "long pole."

**SYNONYM -3:**
**stanga** *f.* • (lit.): bar.

**macello (un)** *exp.* a lot, big-time • (lit.): a slaughter.

example:
Ci divertiremo **un macello** stasera alla festa di carnevale di Lucia!

translation:
We're going to have fun **big-time** tonight at Lucia's carnival party!

---

**mah** *adv.* so-so.

example:
– Come ti senti oggi?
– **Mah**. Stavo meglio la settimana scorsa.

translation:
– How are you doing today?
– **So-so**. Last week I actually felt better.

**NOTE:**
"**Mah**" is also used to mean "I don't know."

---

**mandare qualcuno al diavolo** *exp.* to tell someone to get lost • (lit.): to send someone to the devil.

example:
C'è Roberto. Lui è così fastidioso. Se viene da me, lo **mando al diavolo**!

translation:
There's Roberto. He's so annoying. If he comes up to me, I'm going to tell him **to get lost**!

**SYNONYM -1:**
**Aria!** *interj.* Get lost! • (lit.): air.

**SYNONYM -2:**
**mandare qualcuno a quel paese** *exp.* • (lit.): to send someone to that country.

**SYNONYM -3:**
**mandare qualcuno a fare un bagno** *exp.* • (lit.): to send someone to take a bath.

**SYNONYM -4:**
**Smamma!** *interj.* (from the verb *smammare*, meaning "to beat it") Get lost!

---

**matti (da)** *adv.* big-time • (lit.): from madness (as in "to go mad over something").

example:
– Ti piace la cioccolata?
– **Da matti**!

translation:
– Do you like chocolate?
– **Big-time**!

**SYNONYM -1:**
**alla grande** *exp.* (as introduced in Lesson Five, p. 77) • (lit.): to the big.

**SYNONYM -2:**
**da morire** *adj.* (used to modify a noun or verb – as introduced in Lesson Four, p. 60) big-time • (lit.): to die from.

**SYNONYM -3:**
**della madonna** *exp.* (as introduced in Lesson Two, p. 28) big-time, in a major way • (lit.): of the Madonna.

**SYNONYM -4:**
**il massimo** *exp.* • (lit.): the maximum • *Questa pizza è il massimo!;* This pizza is the best!

---

**megagalattico** *adj.* big-time awesome, fantastic, super cool • (lit.): mega-galactic.

example:
La casa di Elena è **megagalattica**! Ha addirittura una piscina in salotto!

translation:
Elena's house is **awesome**! She even has a swimming pool in her living room!

**NOTE:**
The prefix *mega* can be added to the following single- word synonyms to add emphasis just as "super" or "big-time" does in English.

**SYNONYM -1:**

**boreale** adj. (Northern Italy) • (lit.): borealis.

**SYNONYM -2:**

**cosmico** adj. • (lit.): cosmic.

**NOTE:**

It's interesting to note that in the 1970s, the adjective *cosmic* was used in the United States to mean "fantastic."

**SYNONYM -3:**

**fine del mondo** exp. • (lit.): the end of the world.

**SYNONYM -4:**

**da flash** exp. (from English) • (lit.): from a flash or bulletin (such as a "newsflash").

**SYNONYM -5:**

**galattico** adj. • (lit.): galactic.

**SYNONYM -6:**

**mitico/a** adj. • (lit.): mythical, of mythic proportion.

**SYNONYM -7:**

**mostruoso/a** adj. • (lit.): monstrous.

**SYNONYM -8:**

**pazzesco/a** adj. (Northern & Central Italy) • (lit.): crazy, insane.

**SYNONYM -9:**

**sano/a** adj. • (lit.): sane • It's interesting that in English, the opposite in slang applies: *What an insane car!*

**SYNONYM -10:**

**spaziale** adj. (as introduced in Lesson Three, p. 50) awesome, fantastic • (lit.): spacial.

**mettersi con qualcuno**

exp. to begin a relationship with someone • (lit.): to put oneself with someone.

example:
Ho appena sentito che **ti sei messa con** Alfredo! È vero?

translation:
I just heard that you **started a relationship with** Alfredo! Is that true?

---

**morire dalle risate** exp. to split one's sides with laughter • (lit.): to die from laughter.

example:
That movie was hilarious! I thought I was going **to die laughing**!

translation:
Quel film era buffissimo! Pensavo di **morire dalle risate**!

**VARIATION -1:**

**piegarsi dalle risate** exp. • (lit.): to bend in half from laughter.

**VARIATION -2:**

**sganasciarsi dal ridere** exp. • (lit.): to dislocate one's jaw from laughing.

**VARIATION -3:**

**sganasciarsi dalle risate** exp. • (lit.): to dislocate one's jaw from laughter.

**VARIATION -4:**
**sganasciarsi per le risate** *exp.*
• (lit.): to dislocate one's jaw for laughing.

**non ci piove** *exp.* I'd bet my life on it • (lit.): It's not raining on that.

example:
Il capo ha appena chiamato Pasquale nel suo ufficio. Penso che lo licenzierà. **Non ci piove!**

translation:
The boss just called Pasquale into his office. I think he's going to get fired. **I'd bet my life on it!**

---

**non fare un fico** *exp.* not to do a darn thing, not to do an iota • (lit.): not to do a fig.

example:
Uno di questi giorni Giuseppe verrà licenziato. **Non fa un fico** tutto il giorno!

translation:
One of these days, Giuseppe is going to get fired. He **doesn't do a darn thing** all day!

**SYNONYM:**
**non fare un tubo** *exp.* • (lit.): not to do a pipe.

**non poterne più** *exp.* to be unable to take it any longer • (lit.): not to be able of it any longer.

example:
**Non ne posso più!** Il capo non mi piace e l'orario è lunghissimo! Domani mattina smetto!

translation:
**I can't take it any longer!** I don't like my boss and the hours are terribly long. I'm going to quit in the morning!

---

**nuovo (di)** *adv.* again • (lit.): of new.

example:
Quando ho chiamato Gigi, la linea era occupata. Riproverò **di nuovo** più tardi.

translation:
When I telephoned Gigi, the line was busy. I'll try **again** later.

**Occhio!** *interj.* Watch out! Keep your eyes peeled! • (lit.): Eye!

example:
**Occhio**! Va'piano per queste scale
perchè sono molto ripide.

translation:
**Watch out**! Walk carefully
because these steps are very steep.

---

**okappa** *interj.* (from English) okay.

example:
– Vuoi venire al cinema con me
stasera?
– **Okappa**, ma non posso fare
tardi perchè devo  cominciare a
lavorare presto domattina.

translation:
– Do you want to come with me to
the movies tonight?
– **Okay**, but I can't stay out too
late because I have to
work early in the morning.

**paglia** *f.* cigarette • (lit.): straw.

example:
Alberto ha soltanto dodici anni e
si fa già le **paglie**!

translation:
Alberto is only twelve years old
and he's already smoking
**cigarettes**!

**NOTE:**
**farsi una paglia** *exp.* to
smoke • (lit.): to do oneself a
straw.

**SYNONYM -1:**
**bionda** *f.* a cigarette made from
blond tobacco • (lit.): blond.

**SYNONYM -2:**
**cicca** *f.* (Northern & Central
Italy) • (lit.): from the French
word *chique*, meaning "chewing
tobacco."

---

**osceno/a** *adj.* outrageous,
extraordinary • (lit.): obscene.

example:
Stefania ha detto di aver trovato
una scatola piena di soldi per
strada? È **osceno**!

translation:
Stefania said she found a box full of
money in the street? That's
**outrageous**!

**palla (essere in)** *exp.* to be
in tip-top shape, to be back on
one's feet • (lit.): to be in ball.

example:
Sono stato male per una
settimana, ma ora sono
nuovamente **in palla**!

translation:
I was sick for a week, but I'm
finally **back on my feet**.

**palla** *f.* a bore, a drag • (lit.): bullet, ball.

example:

Ho passato tutta la vacanza al chiuso, perchè non ha fatto altro che piovere. Che **palla**!

translation:

I spent my entire vacation inside because it never stopped raining. My vacation was a **bore**!

**NOTE:**

The literal meaning of **palla** is "ball" which should not be mistaken for the slang meaning of "ball," meaning "a lot of fun" or "a blast." In fact, its meaning is exactly the opposite! For example: *Che palla!* = What a bore! (Not "What a blast!").

**SYNONYM -1:**

**depressione** *f.* said of anything boring and dull • (lit.): depression.

**SYNONYM -2:**

**piaga** *f.* (Northern & Central Italy) • (lit.): plague.

**SYNONYM -3:**

**pizza** *f.*

**ALSO:**

**una palla** / **una balla** *f.* a cock-and-bull story.

---

**pappare** *v.* to eat, to wolf down food • (lit.): from *pappa,* meaning "baby food."

example:

Avevo lasciato un sacco di cibo in frigo, ma Massimo si è **pappato** tutto!

translation:

I had left a lot of food in the refrigerator, but Massimo **ate** it all!

---

**partito/a** *adj.* lost touch with reality • (lit.): left (one's senses).

example:

Farai paracadutismo domani? Ma sei **partito**? È così pericoloso!

translation:

You're going to go skydiving tomorrow? Have you **lost it**? That's so dangerous!

**SYNONYM -1:**

**di fuori (essere)** *exp.* (as introduced in Lesson Two, p. 28) • (lit.): to be out (of one's mind).

**SYNONYM -2:**

**flippato/a** *adj.* • (lit.): flipped.

**SYNONYM -3:**

**fuori di testa (essere)** *exp.* (as introduced in Lesson Seven, p. 118) to be crazy • (lit.): to be out of one's head.

**SYNONYM -4:**

**girare** *v.* (Central Italy) • (lit.): to turn • *Ma ti gira il cervello?;* Are you nuts? (lit.): Is your brain turning?

---

**party** *m.* (borrowed from English) party.

example:

– Tutti, tranne me, sono stati invitati al **party** di Alessandra!

– Forse il tuo invito è andato perduto nella posta.

translation:
– Everyone, but me, was invited to Alessandra's **party**!
– Maybe your invitation got lost in the mail.

---

**pasta d'uomo** *f.* a nice guy, a good egg • (lit.): dough of man.

example:
Mi piace davvero Davide. Ieri mi ha aiutato ad imbiancare tutta la casa. È proprio **una pasta d'uomo**!

translation:
I really like David. He helped me paint my entire house yesterday. He's really a **good egg**!

---

**per carità** *exp.* "please" when used to mean **1.** give me a break, "pah-leeze!"; **2.** "Please, I'm begging you!"; **3.** "Please, that's really not necessary" • (lit.): for charity.

example -1:
– C'è qualcosa in questo negozio che ti piace?
– **Per carità**! Nulla!

translation:
– Is there anything in this store that you like?
– **Give me a break**! Not a thing!

example -2:
**Per carità**. Non dire niente a nessuno!

translation:
**Please, I'm begging you**. Don't tell anyone!

example -3:
– Posso aiutarti a caricare il tuo furgone con la legna?
– No, **per carità**. Non devi!

translation:
– Can I help you load your truck with all this wood?
– No, **please**. You don't have to!

---

**perdere colpi** *exp.* said of someone or something whose performance is diminishing, to go downhill • (lit.): to lose strokes.

example:
Sapevo che Marcello era malato, ma pensavo che stesse meglio. Sono rimasto così sorpreso quando ho saputo che **perdeva colpi**.

translation:
I knew Marcello was sick, but I thought he was doing better. I was so surprised to hear that he's **going downhill**.

---

**pezzi (essere a)** *exp.* to be exhausted (or "to be a nervous wreck" depending on the context) • (lit.): to be in pieces.

example:
Devo schiacciare un sonnellino. Sono **a pezzi**!

translation:
I need to take a nap. I'm **wiped out**!

---

**pizza** *f.* a bore • (lit.): pizza.

example:
Non andare a vedere quel film! L'ho visto ieri ed era una tale **pizza**!

translation:
Don't go see that movie! I saw it yesterday and it was a real **bore**!

**SYNONYM -1:**
**depressione** *f.* said of anything boring and dull • (lit.): depression.

**SYNONYM -2:**
**palla** *f.* (as introduced in Lesson Two, p. 30) a bore, a drag • (lit.): bullet, shot.

**SYNONYM -3:**
**piaga** *f.* (Northern & Central Italy) • (lit.): plague.

---

**portare male gli anni** *exp.*
not to be aging well • (lit.): to carry the years badly.

example:
Martina ha solo venticinque anni? Ne dimostra sessanta! Li **porta davvero male**.

translation:
Martina is only twenty-five years old? She looks about sixty! She's **really not aging well**.

**prendere in castagna** *exp.*
to catch someone in the act •
(lit.): to take in the chestnut.

example:
Ho **preso** Luigi **in castagna**, mentre cercava di rubare la mia bici.

translation:
I **caught Luigi in the act** of trying to steal my bicycle!

**SYNONYM -1:**
**esser colto/a in flagrante** *exp.* • (lit.): to be caught in the flagrant [action].

**SYNONYM -2:**
**esser colto/a sul fatto** *exp.* • (lit.): to be caught in the fact.

---

**prendere qualcuno in giro** *exp.* to pull the wool over someone's eyes (either in a deceitful way or in fun) • (lit.): to take someone for a ride.

example:
Mi sono fidata di Elena, ma per tutto questo tempo mi ha mentito. Non riesco a credere che **mi abbia preso in giro**!

translation:
I really trusted Elena but all this time she was lying to me. I can't believe that she **pulled the wool over my eyes**!

**prendere per i fondelli** *exp.* •
(lit.): to take by the bottom parts.

**prendere per il bavero** *exp.* •
(lit.): to take by the collar.

---

**prof** *m. & f.* professor, teacher •
(lit.): prof.

example:
Hai visto la nostra nuova **prof**? È
bellissima!

translation:
Did you see our new **prof**? She's
absolutely beautiful!

**NOTE:**
Although the academic term for
professor is either **professore** *m.*
or **professoressa** *f.* depending on
the sex, the abbreviated form **prof**
is both masculine and feminine.

---

**protetto/a** *n.* teacher's pet• (lit.):
protected one (from the verb
*proteggere*, meaning "to protect").

example:
L'unico motivo per cui Francesca
prende dei buoni voti è perchè lei è
la **protetta** dell'insegnante.

translation:
The only reason Francesca gets
good grades is because she's the
**teacher's pet**.

**provarci** *v.* to flirt, to hit on
someone • (lit.): from the verb
*provare*, meaning "to try."

example:
Paolo non **ci prova** più con
me, perchè l'ultima volta che
l'ha fatto, l'ho mandato al
diavolo!

translation:
Paolo doesn't **hit on me**
anymore, because the last time
he did, I told him to get lost!

---

**pula (la)** *f.* the police, the
"cops" • (lit.): husk.

example:
Da grande Nicola vuole entrare
nella **pula**.

translation:
When Nicholas grows up, he
wants to be a **cop**.

**piedipiatti** *m.* • (lit.): flat feet.
**NOTE:**
It's interesting to note that the
American equivalent, *flatfoot*,
was an old slang term for "cop."

**sbirro** *m.* • (lit.): from Latin
*birrum*, meaning "hooded
cloak."

**racchia** *f.* said of an extremely ugly girl, a "troll."

example:
Federica è una gran **racchia**, mentre i suoi genitori sono veramente belli!

translation:
Federica is a real **troll**, but her parents are so attractive!

**NOTE:**
This can also be used as an adjective as in *racchio/a*.

---

**ricco sfondato / ricca sfondata (essere)** *exp.* to be filthy rich • (lit.): to be rich without bottom.

example:
Hai visto che macchina cara hanno i genitori di Simona? Devono essere **ricchi sfondati**!

translation:
Did you see the expensive car Simona's parents have? They must be **mega rich**!

---

**rintronato/a** *adj.* said of someone who is rather dull, not too bright, not the sharpest tack on the board • (lit.): from the verb *rintronare,* meaning "to make a loud thunderous noise" (said of someone who looks as if he/she has been stunned from a loud noise or explosion).

example:
Ho provato ad insegnare a Sergio ad usare il computer, ma lui non capisce niente! Deve essere un po' **rintronato**.

translation:
I tried to explain to Sergio how to use the computer, but he just doesn't get it! He's **not the sharpest tack on the board**.

---

**rompi scatole** *m.* annoying person, pain in the butt • (lit.): box-breaker.

example:
Cecilia è così **rompi scatole**! Mi chiama la telefono tutte le volte che ha un problema!

translation:
Cecilia is such a **pain in the butt**. She calls me on the phone every time she has a problem.

**NOTE:**
**scatole** *m.* butt • (lit.): box.

**SYNONYM -1:**
**borsa** *f.* • (lit.): bag.

**SYNONYM -2:**
**mattone** *m.* • (lit.): brick.

**SYNONYM -3:**
**menata** *f.* • annoying thing or situation (not applied to a person).

**SYNONYM -4:**
**palla** *f.* • **1.** an annoying person •
**2.** a bore • (lit.): ball.

**SYNONYM -5:**
**rompimento/a** *n.* • (lit.): a
breaker.

**sacchi** *m.pl.* a multiple of 1,000
lire, equivalent to about 50 cents •
(lit.): sacks (or thousands of lire –
For example: *20 sacchi* = 20,000
lire).

example:
– Quanto hai pagato questa
 bicicletta?
– L'ho pagata 200 **sacchi**!

translation:
– How much did you pay for this
 bike?
– I paid two hundred **thousand
 lire**!

---

**sacco** *m.* a lot, a large quantity •
(lit.): a sack.

example:
Gina ha un **sacco** di soldi. Lei
compra una nuova macchina tutti i
mesi!

translation:
Gina has **a lot** of money. She buys
a new car every month!

**SYNONYM -1:**
**un casino** *m.* • (lit.): a brothel.

**SYNONYM -2:**
**un fracco** *m.* (Northern Italy)

**SYNONYM -3:**
**un frego** *m.* (Central Italy) •
(lit.): from the verb *fregare,*
meaning "to rub" or, in slang, "to
swindle."

**SYNONYM -4:**
**un macello** *m.* • (lit.): a
slaughter.

---

**sbirro** *m.* police officer, cop •
(lit.): from Latin *birrum*, meaning
"hooded cloak."

example:
Corri a trovare uno **sbirro**!
Credo che quell'uomo stia
rapinando quella banca!

translation:
Go run and find a **cop**! I think
that man is robbing that bank!

**SYNONYM -1:**
**piedipiatti** *m.* • (lit.): flat feet.

**SYNONYM -2:**
**pula (la)** *f.* (as introduced in
Lesson Three, p. 51) police
officer, "cop" • (lit.): husk.

---

**sboba** *f.* bad food, "slop."

example:
Hai assaggiato la **sboba** che
Federica ha preparato ieri sera?
Era tremenda!

translation:
Did you taste the **slop** Federica made last night? It was horrible!

**VARIATION:**
**sbobba** *f.*

**scartoffie** *f.pl.* a contemptuous term for schoolbooks, "darned books" • (lit.): old papers.

example:
Devo cancellare la mia vacanza perchè devo leggere tutte queste **scartoffie** entro venerdì prossimo!

translation:
I have to cancel my vacation because I need to read all these **darned books** by next Friday!

**scazzare** *v.* to blow it • (lit.): to "dick" something up.

example:
Ho davvero **scazzato** l'esame! So che non passerò!

translation:
I totally **messed up on** the test! I know I'm not going to pass!

**NOTE:**
This comes from the masculine noun *cazzo*, meaning "penis" or, more closely, "dick." It is included here because of its extreme popularity.

**SYNONYM:**
**fare una cappella** *exp.* • (lit.): to do a mushroom cap.

**scheggiare** *v.* to drive very fast • (lit.): to splinter.

example:
La mia macchina nuova è di grossa cilindrata. Non ti puoi nemmeno immaginare quanto **scheggi**!

translation:
My new car has a lot of power. You won't believe how it can **haul**!

**scocciare qualcuno** *v.* to bug someone • (lit.): to break (an eggshell).

example:
Smettila di farmi tutte queste domande! Mi stai **scocciando**!

translation:
Stop asking me so many questions! You're **bugging** me!

**SYNONYM -1:**
**bombardare qualcuno** *v.* • (lit.): to bombard or shell someone.

**SYNONYM -2:**
**tafanare** *v.* from *tafano*, meaning "horsefly."

**SYNONYM -3:**
**stare sui calli a qualcuno** *exp.* • (lit.): to be on someone's corns.

**scocciarsi** *v.* to be bored • (lit.): to bother oneself.

example:

**Mi** ero così **scocciato** durante la lezione!

translation:

I was really **bored** during the lecture!

**NOTE:**

You may remember that *scocciare* was presented in Lesson Two on page 30. As demonstrated early in its <u>non</u>-reflexive form, *scocciare qualcuno* means "to bug someone." However, in its reflexive form, *scocciarsi* takes on the meaning "to be bored."

**ALSO -1:**

**scocciatore** *m.* / **scocciatrice** *f.* an annoying person • *Che scocciatore quello!;* What a pain in the neck he is!

**ALSO -2:**

**scocciatura** *f.* an annoying task, something that is a pain in the neck to do.

**SYNONYM -1:**

**rompersi** *v.* • (lit.): to break oneself.

**SYNONYM -2:**

**seccarsi** *v.* • (lit.): to dry oneself up.

**SYNONYM -3:**

**stufarsi** *v.*

**NOTE:**

In its non-reflexive form, *stufare* means "to stew." Therefore, *stufarsi* could be loosely translated as "to stew oneself" which is a long, slow, and boring process.

**scorfana** *f.* an extremely ugly woman, a "troll" • (lit.): from *scorfano,* meaning "scorpion fish."

example:

Cinzia era così carina e ora è una **scorfana**! Chissà che le è successo!

translation:

Cinzia used to be so pretty amd now she's a real **troll**! I wonder what happened to her!

**NOTE:**

This term is generally only applied to women.

**SYNONYM:**

**racchia** *f.*

**secchionaccio** *m.* nerdy bookworm.

example:

Fernando non studia mai, mentre suo fratello è un **secchionaccio**.

translation:

Fernando never studies but his brother is a **nerdy bookworm**.

**NOTE:**

The masculine noun **secchionaccio** is a stronger form of **secchione/sechia**, meaning "nerdy, bookworm type."

**segare** *v.* to fail someone • (lit.): to cut with a saw.

example:
Il professore mi ha detto che mi
**sega** alla fine dell'anno, se non
passo il prossimo esame!

translation:
The professor said he would **fail
me** at the end of the school year if
I didn't pass the next test!

**SYNONYM -1:**
**bocciare** *v.* • (lit.): to knock away
the opponent's wood in the game
of bocce.

**SYNONYM -2:**
**fregare** *v.* (Northern & Central
Italy) • (lit.): to rub.

**SYNONYM -3:**
**gambizzare** *v.* (from the feminine
noun *gamba*, meaning "leg" –
therefore the literal translation
could be "to cut someone's legs off
so that he/she can no longer
continue.")

---

**seminare qualcuno** *v.* to ditch
someone • (lit.): to sow or seed
someone.

example:
Il mio fratellino ci veniva dietro da
tutte le parti, ma alla fine lo
abbiamo **seminato** quando siamo
entrati al cinema.

translation:
My little brother was following us
around everywhere, so we finally
**ditched** him when we went to the
movies.

**SYNONYM:**
**tagliare** *v.* • (lit.): to cut.

**NOTE:**
"*Taglia!*" is also used to mean
"Wrap it up!" as in "Wrap up the
conversation!"

---

**sentirsi giù** *exp.* to feel blah •
(lit.): to feel down.

example:
**Mi sento giù** oggi. Penso di
rimanere a casa a leggere.

translation:
I **feel blah** today. I think I'll just
stay home and read.

**SYNONYM:**
**sgasato/a** *adj.* • (lit.): from the
verb *sgasarsi*, meaning "to let
the gas out."

---

**sfacchinare** *v.* to work hard •
(lit.): to work hard like a porter
(from the masculine noun
*facchino*, meaning "porter").

example:
Ho **sfacchinato** per sei mesi e
il mio capo mi ha licenziato
soltanto perchè sono arrivato
tardi ieri!

translation:
I **worked really hard** for six
months and my boss fired me
because I come in late
yesterday!

**SYNONYM:**
**sgobbare** *v.* to work hard
(from *gobba*, meaning "hump,"
representing a heavy load being
carried on one's shoulders or
back).

**sgasarsi** *v.* to come off one's high horse.

example:
Luigi crede di essere troppo ganzo, ma non lo è. Lui deve cercare di **sgasarsi**!

translation:
Luigi thinks he is way too cool, but he's not. He should try to **come off his high horse**!

---

**sgobbare** *v.* to work hard (from *gobba,* meaning "hump," representing a heavy load being carried on one's shoulders or back).

example:
Mi piacerebbe andare al cinema con te, ma devo **sgobbare** tutta la notte. Devo presentare una grossa relazione domani mattina.

translation:
I'd like to go with you to the movies, but I have **to work hard** all night. I'm giving a big presentation tomorrow morning.

**NOTE:**
**sgobbo** *m.* work • *andare allo sgobbo;* to go to work.

---

**sgommare** *f.* (said of a car) to peel out with the scretching of tires • (lit.): to make tires or "to make tracks."

example:
Non appena è scattato il verde, Marco è partito **sgommando** con la sua Ferrari nuova di zecca.

translation:
As soon as the light turned green, Marco **peeled out** in his brand new Ferrari.

**NOTE:**
**gomma** *f.* tire.

---

**sgranocchiare** *v.* to eat • (lit.): to munch, to nibble.

example:
Hai sempre fame? Ma se hai **sgranocchiato** tutto il giorno!

translation:
You're still hungry? You've been **eating** all day!

---

**sgrifare** *v.* to wolf down food • (lit.): to snort.

example:
Hai visto come Roberta ha **sgrifato** tutta quella torta? Che schifo!

translation:
Did you see Roberta **wolf down** that entire pie? It was disgusting!

**SYNONYM -1:**
**pappare** *v.* • (lit.): from *pappa,* meaning "baby food."

**SYNONYM -2:**
**sbafare** *v.* • (lit.): from *sbafo,* meaning "a meal that one eats without paying for it."

**SYNONYM -3:**
**spazzolare** *v.* • (lit.): to brush.

**SYNONYM -4:**

**strafognarsi** *v.* • (lit.): from *fogna,* meaning "sewer."

---

**spappolare** *v.* to kill• (lit.): to crush or crumble.

example:

Mentre attraversavo la strada, un autista è passato col rosso e per poco non mi **spappolava**!

translation:

As I was walking across the street, a driver ran the red light and almost **killed** me!

---

**spararsi** *v.* to partake, to treat oneself to something • (lit.): to shoot oneself.

example:

Dopo cena **mi sparo** un po' di musica e poi me ne vado a letto.

translation:

After dinner, I'm going **to enjoy** a little music and then I'm going to bed.

---

**spaziale** *adj.* awesome, fantastic • (lit.): spacial.

example:

Che bel vestito! È davvero **spaziale**!

translation:

What a great dress! It's **awesome**!

**SYNONYM -1:**

**boreale** *adj.* (Northern Italy) • (lit.): borealis.

**SYNONYM -2:**

**cosmico** *adj.* • (lit.): cosmic • It's interesting to note that in the 1970s, *cosmic* was a popular term in the United States, meaning "fantastic."

**SYNONYM -3:**

**fine del mondo** *exp.* • (lit.): the end of the world.

**SYNONYM -4:**

**da flash** *exp.* (from English) • (lit.): from a flash or bulletin (such as a "newsflash").

**SYNONYM -5:**

**galattico** *adj.* • (lit.): galactic.

**SYNONYM -6:**

**il massimo/la massima** *adj.* • (lit.): the maximum.

**SYNONYM -7:**

**mitico/a** *adj.* • (lit.): mythical, of mythic proportion.

**SYNONYM -8:**

**mostruoso/a** *adj.* • (lit.): monstrous.

**SYNONYM -9:**

**pazzesco/a** *adj.* (Northern & Central Italy) • (lit.): crazy, insane.

**SYNONYM -10:**

**sano/a** *adj.* • (lit.): sane • It's interesting that in English, the opposite in slang applies: *What an _insane_ car!*

**SYNONYM -11:**

**tosto/a** *adj.* • (lit.): toasted.

**SYNONYM -12:**

**troppo** *adj.* • (lit.): too much.

**spennare** v. to swindle, to fleece
• (lit.): to pluck.

example:
Ho mangiato in un ristorante caro, dove mi hanno **spennato**!

translation:
I ate in an expensive restaurant where I got **fleeced**!

**VARIATION:**

**spennato/a** adj. broke • (lit.): unfeathered.

---

**spremersi le meningi** exp. to rack one's brain • (lit.): to wring one's brain (from the Greek word meninx, meaning "brain").

example:
Come si chiama tua sorella? Ho **spremuto invano le mie meningi** per cercare di ricordarlo!

translation:
What is your sister's name? I've been **racking my brain** trying to remember it!

**SYNONYM:**

**rompersi la testa** exp. • (lit.): to break one's head.

---

**sputtanare** v. to blow money, to throw money away • (lit.): from puttana, meaning "whore."

example:
Enrico compra tutto quelo che vede. **Sputtana** così tanti soldi in un sol giorno!

translation:
Enrico buys everything he sees. He **blows so much money** in just one day!

---

**stoppare** v. (from English, most commonly used in soccer) to stop.

example -1:
Ronaldo ha **stoppato** il pallone, ha calciato, e ha segnato un bel goal.

translation:
Ronaldo **stopped** the ball, kicked it, and scored a beautiful goal.

example -2:
**Stoppa**! Hai quasi arrotato un pedone. Fa'attenzione!

translation:
**Stop**! You almost ran over that pedestrian. Be careful!

---

**stracci** m.pl. old clothes, "threads" • (lit.): rags.

example:
Hai visto che **stracci** aveva addosso Chiara a scuola? Stava malissimo!

translation:
Did you see the **clothes** Chiara was wearing in school? She looked terrible!

---

**strappo** m. a ride, a lift • (lit.): a tear.

example:
Vuoi che ti dia uno **strappo** al mercato?

translation:
Would you like me to give you a **lift** to the market?

---

**strizzacervelli** m. (humorous) psychoanalyst, "shrink" • (lit.): from strizzare, meaning "to squeeze," and cervelli, meaning "brains."

example:
- Mia zia pensa di essere una gallina.
- Perchè non la mandi da uno **strizzacervelli**?
- Perchè abbiamo bisogno delle uova!

translation:
- My aunt thinks she's a chicken!
- Why don't you sent her to a **shrink**?
- Because we need the eggs!

---

**stronzo** m. despicable person, jerk • (lit.): turd.

example:
Quello **stronzo** ha appena rotto la mia finestra con un sasso!

translation:
That **jerk** just broke my window with a rock!

**SYNONYM -1:**
**cretino/a** n. • (lit.): cretin.

**SYNONYM -2:**
**fesso/a** n. jerk, dimwit, dolt, fool • (lit.): from the verb fendere, meaning "to split" – a rough

translation could be "someone who is split in the head" or "someone who has half a brain."

**VARIATION:**
**stronzetto** m. (diminutive form of stronzo) little jerk.

---

**succhiare** v. (said of a car) to guzzle gas • (lit.): to suck.

example:
Hai finito di nuovo la benzina? Non ho mai visto una macchina che **succhia** quanto la tua!

translation:
You ran out of gas again? I've never seen a car that **guzzles** the way yours does!

**SYNONYM -1:**
**bere** v. • (lit.): to drink.

**ALSO:**
**Questa non la bevo!** exp. I don't believe that! • (lit.): I'm not drinking (swallowing) that!

**SYNONYM -2:**
**poppare** v. • (lit.): to suck (from the feminine noun poppa, meaning "breast").

---

**succhiotto** m. hickey • (lit.): (from the verb succhiare, meaning "to suck") a "sucked thing."

example:
Simona ieri sera è tornata a casa con un **succhiotto** sul collo! Immagino che si sia divertita con Roberto!

translation:
Simona came home last night with a **hickey** on her neck! I guess she had a good time with Roberto!

---

**sull'anima (stare)** *exp.* to annoy, to get on someone's nerves • (lit.): to be on one's soul.

example:
Il nuovo impiegato **mi sta davvero sull'anima**! Non sta mai zitto!

translation:
The new employee is really **getting on my nerves**! He never shuts up!

**SYNONYM -1:**
**stare sui calli a qualcuno** *exp.* • (lit.): to stand on someone's corns.

**SYNONYM -2:**
**scassare** *v.* • (lit.): to unpack.

**SYNONYM -3:**
**tafanare** *v.* • (lit.): from *tafano*, meaning "horsefly" (insinuating that someone is as annoying as a huge fly).

---

**super bono/a** *adj.* super good-looking, gorgeous • (lit.): super good.

example:
Marco è **super bono** ed io sono innamorata pazza di lui, ma purtroppo io non gli piaccio affatto.

translation:
Marco is **super hot** and I'm desperately in love with him, but unfortunately he doesn't like me at all.

**tappo grasso** *m.* short, fat guy • (lit.): fat cork.

example:
Davide e Alessio sono gemelli, ma Alessio è un gigante e Davide è un **tappo grasso**!

translation:
David and Alessio are twins, but Alessio is a giant and David is a **short, fat guy**!

**SYNONYM -1:**
**ciccio bomba** *m.* • (lit.): fat bomb.

**SYNONYM -2:**
**ciccione/a** *n.* fatty, tubby.

---

**testa di rapa** *exp.* nerd, geek, jerk • (lit.): beet head.

example:
Hai visto il tipo con cui Angela è uscita ieri sera? Angela ha detto che si è sporcato tre volte durante la cena. Che **testa di rapa**!

translation:
Did you see the guy Angela went out with last night? Angela said that he got stuff on himself three times during dinner! What a **nerd**!

**tipo** *m.* guy, "dude" • (lit.): type, species.

example:
Conosci quel **tipo**? Io non l'ho mai visto prima.

translation:
Do you know that **guy**? I've never seen him before.

**NOTE:**

**tipa** *f.* girl, "chick" • (lit.): type, species.

**tirare qualcuno** *v.* to attract or "grab" someone • (lit.): to pull.

example:
**Ti tira** questo vestito? Mi piace un sacco!

translation:
How does this dress **grab you**? Personally, I love it!

**tirare un bidone** *exp.* to stand someone up on a date • (lit.): to throw a trash can.

example:
Ho aspettato Alessio per un'ora! Credo che mi abbia **tirato un bidone**!

translation:
I've been waiting an hour for Alessio to arrive! I think he **stood me up**!

**VARIATION:**
**fare un bidone** *exp.* • (lit.): to do/to make a trash can.

**SYNONYM:**
**dare buca** *exp.* • (lit.): to give hole.

**tirare** *v.* to smoke • (lit.): to pull (a puff of smoke).

example:
Da quanto è che **tiri**? Non sai che ti fa male?

translation:
How long have you been **smoking**? Don't you know it's bad for your health?

**VARIATION:**
**fare un tiro** *exp.* to take a puff of a cigarette • (lit.): to make a pull.

**tirato/a** *adj.* dressed up • (lit.): pulled (together).

example:
Stai benissimo! Non ti avevo mai visto così **tirato**!

translation:
You look great! I've never seen you so **dressed up** before!

**topaia** *f.* horrible dwelling, "rat-trap" • (lit.): small mouse hole (from the masculine noun *topo*, meaning "mouse").

example:
Giovanni sta spendendo una fortuna per il suo nuovo appartamento, che è soltanto una **topaia**!

translation:
Giovanni is paying a fortune for his new apartment, which is really a **dump**!

---

**trampoli** *m.pl.* high heels • (lit.): stilts.

example:
Hai visto che **trampoli** portava Giovanna oggi? Sembrava un gigante!

translation:
Did you see the **high heels** Giovanna was wearing today? She looked like a giant!

**NOTE:**
**Trompoli** is also used to mean "long and thin legs."

---

**troiaio** *m.* pigsty • (lit.): from *troia*, meaning "sow."

example:
Hai visto l'appartamento di Marco? È un **troiaio**!

translation:
Did you see Marco's apartment? It's a **pigsty**!

**ubriaco fradicio** *exp.* roaring drunk • (lit.): soaking wet drunk.

example:
Giovanni ha bevuto soltanto una birra ed è già **ubriaco fradicio**!

translation:
Giovanni only had one beer and he's already **roaring drunk**!

**SYNONYM -1:**
**bere come una spugna** *exp.* to drink an excessive amount of alcohol • (lit.): to drink like a sponge.

**SYNONYM -2:**
**bevuto/a** *adj.* • (lit.): the past tense of *bevere*, meaning "to drink."

**SYNONYM -3:**
**inzupparsi** *v.* to get drunk • (lit.): to get soaked.

---

**ultima** *f.* news • (lit.): last (or the "latest").

example:
Hai sentito l'**ultima**? Massimo si sposa la prossima settimana!

translation:
Did you hear the **news**? Massimo is getting married next week!

# V

**vecchi** *m.pl.* parents, "folks" • (lit.): old people.

example:
Vado a Firenze per passare le vacanze con i miei **vecchi**.

translation:
I'm going to Florence to spend the holiday with my **folks**.

**NOTE:**
**vecchio** *m.* father • (lit.): old man / **vecchia** *f.* mother • (lit.): old lady.

---

**venir alle mani** *exp.* to get into a fistfight, to come to blows • (lit.): to come to hands.

example:
Invece di risolvere il problema da persone mature, Ernesto e Simone sono **venuti alle mani** per una stupidaggine!

translation:
Instead of having a mature discussion, Ernesto and Simone **got into a fistfight** over something really stupid!

**SYNONYM -1:**
**fare a cazzotti** *exp.* • (lit.): to do punches.

**SYNONYM -2:**
**piallare** *v.* to flatten someone • (lit.): to plane.

---

**vita (essere una)** *exp.* to be a long time • (lit.): to be a life(time).

example:
È **una vita** che non ti vedo! Come stai?

translation:
It's been **such a long time** since I've seen you! How are you?

# ORDER FORM

## SLANGMAN PUBLISHING

12206 Hillslope Street
Studio City, CA 91604 • USA

INTERNATIONAL:
**1-818-769-1914**

TOLL FREE (US/Canada):
**1-877-SLANGMAN**
**(1-877-752-6462)**

Worldwide FAX:
**1-413-647-1589**

*Get the latest news, preview chapters, and shop online at:*

**WWW.SLANGMAN.COM**

## SHIPPING

—Domestic Orders—

**SURFACE MAIL**
(delivery time 5-7 days).
Add $4 shipping/handling
for the first item, $1 for
each additional item.

**RUSH SERVICE**
Available at extra charge.
Please telephone us for
details.

—International Orders—

**OVERSEAS SURFACE**
(delivery time 6-8 weeks).
Add $5 shipping/handling
for the first item, $2 for
each additional item.

**OVERSEAS AIRMAIL**
Available at extra charge.
Please phone for details.

| PRODUCT | TYPE | PRICE | QTY | TOTAL |
|---|---|---|---|---|
| **AMERICAN SLANG & IDIOMS** | | | | |
| **STREET SPEAK 1:** *Complete Course in American Slang & Idioms* | book | $18.95 | | |
| | cassette | $12.50 | | |
| **STREET SPEAK 2:** *Complete Course in American Slang & Idioms* | book | $21.95 | | |
| | cassette | $12.50 | | |
| **STREET SPEAK 3:** *Complete Course in American Slang & Idioms* | book | $21.95 | | |
| | cassette | $12.50 | | |
| **SPANISH SLANG & IDIOMS** | | | | |
| **STREET SPANISH 1:** *The Best of Spanish Slang* | book | $15.95 | | |
| | cassette | $12.50 | | |
| **STREET SPANISH 2:** *The Best of Spanish Idioms* | book | $15.95 | | |
| | cassette | $12.50 | | |
| **STREET SPANISH 3:** *The Best of Naughty Spanish* | book | $15.95 | | |
| | cassette | $12.50 | | |
| **STREET SPANISH DICTIONARY & THESAURUS** | book | $16.95 | | |
| **FRENCH SLANG & IDIOMS** | | | | |
| **STREET FRENCH 1:** *The Best of French Slang* | book | $15.95 | | |
| | cassette | $12.50 | | |
| **STREET FRENCH 2:** *The Best of French Idioms* | book | $15.95 | | |
| | cassette | $12.50 | | |
| **STREET FRENCH 3:** *The Best of Naughty French* | book | $15.95 | | |
| | cassette | $12.50 | | |
| **STREET FRENCH DICTIONARY & THESAURUS** | book | $16.95 | | |
| **ITALIAN SLANG & IDIOMS** | | | | |
| **STREET ITALIAN 1:** *The Best of Italian Slang* | book | $15.95 | | |
| | cassette | $12.50 | | |
| **STREET ITALIAN 2:** *The Best of Naughty Italian* — Available Nov 2000 | book | $15.95 | | |
| | cassette | $12.50 | | |
| **Total for Merchandise** | | | | |
| **Sales Tax** *(California Residents Only add 8.25%)* | | | | |
| **Shipping** *(See Left)* | | | | |
| **ORDER TOTAL** | | | | |

*prices subject to change*

Name _____

(School/Company) _____

Street Address _____

City _____ State/Province _____ Postal Code _____

Country _____ Phone _____ Email _____

### METHOD OF PAYMENT (CHECK ONE)

☐ Personal Check or Money Order *(Must be in U.S. funds and drawn on a U.S. bank.)*
☐ VISA          ☐ Master Card          ☐ Discover

| | | | | | | | | | | | | | | | |
|--|--|--|--|--|--|--|--|--|--|--|--|--|--|--|--|

Credit Card Number

Expiration Date

▲ **Signature** *(important!)*

**PLEASE SEE ORDER FORM ON OTHER SIDE!**